ROUTLEDGE LIBRARY EDITIONS: HINDUISM

Volume 7

THE LOVES OF KRISHNA

THE LOVES OF KRISHNA
In Indian Painting and Poetry

W. G. ARCHER

LONDON AND NEW YORK

First published in 1957 by George Allen & Unwin Ltd

This edition first published in 2019
by Routledge
2 Park Square, Milton Park, Abingdon, Oxon OX14 4RN

and by Routledge
52 Vanderbilt Avenue, New York, NY 10017

Routledge is an imprint of the Taylor & Francis Group, an informa business

© 1957 George Allen & Unwin Ltd

All rights reserved. No part of this book may be reprinted or reproduced or utilised in any form or by any electronic, mechanical, or other means, now known or hereafter invented, including photocopying and recording, or in any information storage or retrieval system, without permission in writing from the publishers.

Trademark notice: Product or corporate names may be trademarks or registered trademarks, and are used only for identification and explanation without intent to infringe.

British Library Cataloguing in Publication Data
A catalogue record for this book is available from the British Library

ISBN: 978-0-367-14300-8 (Set)
ISBN: 978-0-429-05711-3 (Set) (ebk)
ISBN: 978-0-367-14791-4 (Volume 7) (hbk)
ISBN: 978-0-367-14799-0 (Volume 7) (pbk)
ISBN: 978-0-429-05345-0 (Volume 7) (ebk)

Publisher's Note
The publisher has gone to great lengths to ensure the quality of this reprint but points out that some imperfections in the original copies may be apparent.

Disclaimer
The publisher has made every effort to trace copyright holders and would welcome correspondence from those they have been unable to trace.

THE LOVES
OF KRISHNA

IN INDIAN PAINTING
AND POETRY

by

W. G. ARCHER

LONDON
GEORGE ALLEN & UNWIN LTD
Ruskin House Museum Street

FIRST PUBLISHED IN 1957

This book is copyright under the Berne Convention. Apart from any fair dealing for the purposes of private study, research, criticism or review, as permitted under the Copyright Act, 1911, no portion may be reproduced by any process without written permission. Enquiry should be made to the publisher.

PRINTED IN GREAT BRITAIN
in 11 point Baskerville type
BY UNWIN BROTHERS LIMITED
WOKING AND LONDON

TO
MR. AND MRS. H. N.
WITH LOVE
AND ADMIRATION

Radha and Krishna in the Grove
Kangra (Punjab Hills), c.1785

ACKNOWLEDGMENTS

I am deeply indebted to Dr. A. L. Basham for generous guidance throughout the preparation of this book, to George Keyt for permitting me to quote extensively from his brilliant translation of the *Gita Govinda*, and to Deben Bhattacharya who supplied me with new translations of later poems and discussed a number of important points. I must also express my deep gratitude to Mildred Archer and to Gopi Krishna Kanoria for valued criticism and advice, to Messrs. Faber and Faber, the Harvill Press, Messrs. Macmillan, the Oxford University Press, the Phoenix House and Messrs. Sidgwick and Jackson for permitting me to quote passages from works still copyright, to Professor J. Brough for an informative note on Bhanu Datta's *Rasamanjari* and to all those owners of collections who have either allowed me to reproduce pictures in their possession or have kindly supplied me with photographs.

Part of the material for this book was delivered as lectures to the Royal Asiatic Society, the Royal India, Pakistan and Ceylon Society and at the Victoria and Albert Museum.

CONTENTS

ACKNOWLEDGMENTS	page 9
I INTRODUCTION	13
II THE MAHABHARATA: KRISHNA THE HERO	17
III THE BHAGAVATA PURANA: THE COWHERD	26
i *Birth and Early Adventures*	
ii *The Loves of the Cowgirls*	
iii *The Death of the Tyrant*	
IV THE BHAGAVATA PURANA: THE PRINCE	49
i *The Return to Court*	
ii *Marriages and Offspring*	
iii *Last Phases*	
iv *The* Purana *Re-considered*	
V THE KRISHNA OF POETRY	72
i *The Triumph of Radha*	
ii *The* Gita Govinda	
iii *Later Poetry*	
iv *The* Rasika Priya	
VI THE KRISHNA OF PAINTING	93
NOTES	115
BIBLIOGRAPHY	121
INDEX	123
PLATES AND COMMENTARY	129

I
INTRODUCTION

During the twentieth century, a certain type of Indian painting began to fascinate the West. Unlike Mughal art, it was a product of Hindu courts in Rajasthan and the Punjab Hills and unlike Mughal painting, its chief concern was with the varied phases of romance. Ladies would be shown brooding in their chambers as storm clouds mounted in the sky. A girl might be portrayed desperately fondling a plantain tree, gripping a pet falcon, the symbol of her lover, or hurrying through the rainy darkness intent only on reaching a longed-for tryst. A prince would appear lying on a terrace, his outstretched arms striving vainly to detain a calm beauty or welcoming with delight a bashful girl as she slowly advanced. In all these pictures, romantic love was treated as the highest good and physical passion was interpreted with a freshness and innocence unequalled in the world's art.

Such paintings were, at first sight, easy to appreciate. Although they alternated between two methods of expression—the first a style of savage distortion, the second a style of the softest grace—each manner enlivened the common subject.[1] Yet in two respects elucidation was vitally necessary. Just as in Japan, the lover might express his longings by cryptic references to Nature, the Indian artist employed poetic symbols to charge his subjects with romantic ardour. Flowers were never merely flowers nor clouds clouds. The symbols of Indian poetry—the lotus swaying in a stream, the flowering creeper embracing a trunk—were intended to suggest passion-haunted ladies. The mingling of clouds, rain and lightning symbolized the embraces of lovers, and commonplace objects such as dishes, vases, ewers and lamps were brought into subtle conjunction to hint at 'the right true end of love.' What, in fact, might seem at first sight to be a simple portrait, proved on closer understanding to be a study in despair, a revelation of delight or a clue to rapture, each image with its sexual implications contriving to express some nuance of longing. In these pictures, only a part of the meaning was apparent and without a comprehension of the poetry, much of its true significance was lost.

[1] Note 1.

Such an obstacle to understanding was real enough but, as the eye ranged over this new kind of love-painting, a second difficulty appeared. In many pictures, the lover had special characteristics. He was shown with a crown of peacock's feathers, clad in a golden *dhoti* and in every case his skin was mauve or slate-blue.[1] In certain cases, the lady of his choice appeared bowing at his feet, her pose suggesting the deepest adoration; yet, in other pictures, his role was quite different. He was then a resolute warrior, fighting and destroying demons. It was clear, in fact, that here was no ordinary lover but one who might also be a god. At the same time, other perplexing circumstances were present. The lover's appearance was that of an aristocratic youth and the ladies whom he loved had the bearing of elegant princesses. Yet often the scene of their encounters was a forest thick with flowering trees. His companions were cowherds and the objects of his love were not the ladies of a court but cow-girls. Other activities betrayed the same lowly sphere. In certain pictures, he was shown eating with cowherds, sharing in their sports, grazing the cattle and himself milking cows. That such a lover should dominate the paintings was perplexing in the extreme and just as cultured Indians would be baffled by Italian and Flemish painting unless they already knew the life of Christ, it was clear that part, even the majority, of these pictures would remain obscure unless the character of their central figure was first explained. One further point remained. In many cases, the pictures were not intended to be viewed in isolation but were illustrations of a text. Many were inscribed with Sanskrit or Hindi verses and in each case there was an intimate connection between the content of the picture and the poem's subject. To understand the pictures, therefore, some acquaintance with these texts was necessary for only in this way could the identity and role of the blue-skinned lover be appreciated. He was, in fact, Krishna—an incarnation of God—and in his worship some of the deepest requirements of the Indian spirit found ecstatic release.

The purpose of this book is to throw some light on Indian painting by presenting the story of Krishna in the clearest possible terms. It might be supposed that, of all Indian gods, Krishna was already the one best known to the West and therefore, perhaps, the one least requiring explanation. Among modern poets, Sacheverell Sitwell devotes a whole poem in *Canons of Giant Art* to describing Krishna's effect.

[1] Note 2.

INTRODUCTION

> Rain falls and ceases, all the forest trembles:
> Mystery walks the woods once more,
> We hear a flute.
> It moves on earth, it is the god who plays
> With the flute to his lips and music in his breath:
> The god is Krishna in his lovely youth.

Louis MacNeice in *Ten Burnt Offerings* describes a much-loved cat,

> Fluid as Krishna chasing the milkmaids.

And the same Krishna, flute player and lover of milkmaids, is familiar to British audiences from the dancing of Ram Gopal. Yet side by side with this magnetic figure, a second, strangely different Krishna is also known. This second Krishna is the preacher of the *Bhagavad Gita*, the great sermon delivered on the battlefield of Kurukshetra. It is a cardinal document of Indian ethics, and consoled Mahatma Gandhi during his work for Indian independence. It has for many years been known in the West but has recently attracted fresh attention through a modern translation by Christopher Isherwood and Swami Prabhavananda. This Krishna of the *Gita* is clearly quite different in character from the Krishna of the milkmaids and, without some effort at reconciliation, the two must obviously present a baffling enigma. Indeed so great is the contrast that many Englishmen, entranced by the lover, might be astonished to hear of a more didactic role, while those who value the *Gita* might easily be disturbed on finding its author so daringly identified with the theory and practice of romantic love. The truth, if we are to admit it, is that despite considerable acquaintance with Krishna as a name, few educated people in the West have intimate knowledge of his story. In fact, we have only to ask some basic questions to realize how slender is general understanding. What, for example, were the circumstances in which Krishna was born and why did he enter the world? Of which Indian god is he an incarnation? Who were his parents and how did he come to live among cowherds? Who were Radha and Rukmini? In what ways did he love the milkmaids and why has this aspect of his story assumed such big proportions in Indian religion? Why, in fact, is God a romantic lover? Just as few Indians, even highly educated Indians, could survive a friendly cross-examination on details of the New Testament, the majority of cultured Englishmen would find it hard to answer even a few of these simple questions.

It is to remedy in part this situation that I have marshalled the material given in this book. With certain types of issue I have made no attempt to deal. I have not, for example, discussed statements such as 'Krishna was not a god but a hero of a rough tribe of cowherds.' 'The Gita is an interpolation.' 'There is general agreement on the historicity of Krishna.' 'Radha appears to be a late addition.' Higher Criticism, whether applied to the Bible or to the classics of Indian religion must necessarily remain a small scholars' preserve—of vital importance to the few but of little account to the main body of believers or to artists illustrating adored themes. I have rather been concerned to present information about Krishna in the form in which it has actually reached Indian minds and has influenced belief and worship. During the last two thousand years, various texts have dealt with Krishna, emphasizing first one and then another aspect of his character and in the process assembling more and more details. These texts are still revered by Indians and although they are the product of widely separated eras, all of them have still an air of contemporary authority. By considering them in historical sequence, we can understand not only the subject-matter of romantic Indian painting but realize why Krishna, the adored lover, should still enchant religious India.

II

THE *MAHABHARATA:* KRISHNA THE HERO

The first reference to Krishna occurs in the *Chandogya Upanishad* of perhaps the sixth century B.C. *Upanishads* were 'forest sittings' or 'sessions with teachers.' Sages and their disciples discussed the nature of life and strove to determine the soul's exact relationship to God. The starting-point was the theory of re-incarnation. Death, it was believed, did not end the soul. Death was merely a stepping-stone to another life, the soul moving from existence to existence in one long effort to escape re-birth. From this cycle, only one experience could bring release and that was consciousness or actual knowledge of the supreme Spirit. When that state was achieved, the soul blended with the Godhead and the cycle ended. The problem of problems, therefore, was how to attain such knowledge. The *Chandogya Upanishad* does not offer any startling solution to this matter. The teacher who conducts the session is a certain Ghora of the Angirasa family and it is the person of his disciple rather than his actual message which concerns us. The disciple is called Krishna and his mother has the name Devaki. Devaki is the later Krishna's mother and there is accordingly every reason to suppose that the two Krishnas are the same. Nothing, however, is stated of this early Krishna's career and although parts of the sage's teachings have been compared to passages in the *Gita*,[1] Krishna himself remains a vague and dim name.

For the next few centuries, knowledge of Krishna remains in this fragmentary state. Nothing further is recorded and not until the great Indian epic, the *Mahabharata*, crystallizes out between the fourth century B.C. and the fourth century A.D. does a more detailed Krishna make his appearance.[2] By the end of this period, many vital changes had taken place. The Indian world-view had become much clearer and it is possible not only to connect Krishna with a definite character but to see him in clear relation to cosmic events. The supreme Spirit was now envisaged as a single all-powerful God, known according to his functions as Brahma, Vishnu and Siva. As Brahma, he brought into existence three worlds—heaven, earth and the nether regions—and also created gods or lesser divinities, earth

[1] Note 3.   [2] Note 4.

and nature spirits, demons, ogres and men themselves. Siva, for his part, was God the final dissolver or destroyer, the source of reproductive energy and the inspirer of asceticism. He was thought of in many forms—as a potent ascetic, a butcher wild for blood, a serene dancer—and in his character of regenerator was represented by his symbol, the *lingam* or phallus. The third aspect, Vishnu, was God in his character of loving protector and preserver. This great Trinity was ultimately supreme but under it were a number of lesser powers. Those that represented the forces of good were called *devas* or gods. They were led by their king, Indra, lord of clouds, and associated with him were gods such as Agni (fire), Varuna (water), Surya the sun and Kama the god of passion. These gods lived in Indra's heaven, a region above the world but lower than Vaikuntha, the heaven of Vishnu. Dancing-girls and musicians lived with them and the whole heaven resembled a majestic court on earth. From this heaven the gods issued from time to time intervening in human affairs. Demons, on the other hand, were their exact opposites. They represented powers of evil, were constantly at war with the gods and took vicious pleasure in vexing or annoying the good. Below gods and demons were men themselves.

In this three-tiered universe, transmigration of souls was still the basic fact but methods of obtaining release were now much clearer. A man was born, died and then was born again. If he acted well, did his duty and worked ceaselessly for good, he followed what was known as the path of *dharma* or righteousness. This ensured that at each succeeding birth he would start a stage more favourably off than in his previous existence till, by sheer goodness of character, he qualified for admission to Indra's heaven and might even be accounted a god. The achievement of this status, however, did not complete his cycle, for the ultimate goal still remained. This was the same as in earlier centuries—release from living by union with or absorption into the supreme Spirit; and only when the individual soul had reached this stage was the cycle of birth and re-birth completed. The reverse of this process was illustrated by the fate of demons. If a man lapsed from right living, his second state was always worse than his first. He might then be born in humble surroundings or if his crimes were sufficiently great, he became a demon. As such, his capacity for evil was greatly increased and his chances of ultimate salvation correspondingly worsened. Yet even for demons, the ultimate goal was the same—release from living and blissful identification with the Supreme.

Dharma alone, however, could not directly achieve this end. This could be done by the path of *yoga* or self-discipline—a path which involved penances, meditation and asceticism. By ridding his mind of all desires and attachments, by concentrating on pure abstractions, the ascetic 'obtained insight which no words could express. Gradually plumbing the cosmic mystery, his soul entered realms far beyond the comparatively tawdry heavens where the great gods dwelt in light and splendour. Going "from darkness to darkness deeper yet," he solved the mystery beyond all mysteries; he understood, fully and finally, the nature of the universe and of himself and he reached a realm of truth and bliss, beyond birth and death. And with this transcendent knowledge came another realization—he was completely, utterly, free. He had found ultimate salvation, the final triumph of the soul.'[1] Such a complete identification with the supreme Spirit, however, was not easily come by and often many existences were required before the yogi could achieve this sublime end.

There remained a third way—the path of *bhakti* or devotion to God. If a man loved God not as an abstract spirit but as a loving Person, if he loved with intensity and singleness of heart, adoration itself might obtain for him the same reward as a succession of good lives. Vishnu as protector might reward love with love and confer immediately the blessing of salvation.

The result, then, was that three courses were now open to a man and whether he followed one or other depended on his own particular cast of mind, the degree of his will-power, the strength of his passions and finally, his capacity for renunciation, righteousness and love. On these qualifications the upshot would largely depend. But they were not the only factors. Since gods and demons were part of the world, a man could be aided or frustrated according as gods or demons chose to intervene. Life could, in fact, be viewed from two angles. On the one hand it was one long effort to blend with the Godhead—an effort which only the individual could make. On the other hand, it was a war between good and evil, gods and demons; and to such a contest, God as Vishnu could not remain indifferent. While the forces of evil might properly be allowed to test or tax the good, they could never be permitted completely to win the day. When, therefore, evil appeared to be in the ascendant, Vishnu intervened and corrected the balance. He took flesh and entering the world, slew demons, heartened the righteous and from time to time conferred salvation by directly exempting individuals from further re-births.

It is these beliefs which govern the *Mahabharata* epic and provide

[1] A. L. Basham, *The Wonder that was India*, 245.

the clue to Krishna's role. Its prime subject is a feud between two families, a feud which racks and finally destroys them. At the same time, it is very much more. Prior to the events narrated in the text, Vishnu has already undergone seven incarnations, taking the forms of a fish, tortoise, boar and man-lion and later those of Vamana the dwarf, Parasurama ('Rama with the Axe'), and finally, the princely Rama. In each of these incarnations, he has intervened and, for the time being, rectified the balance. During the period covered by the epic, he undergoes an eighth incarnation and it is in connection with this supremely vital intervention that Krishna appears.

To understand the character which now unfolds, we must briefly consider the central story of the *Mahabharata*. This is narrated in the most baffling and stupendous detail. Cumbrous names confront us on every side while digressions and sub-plots add to the general atmosphere of confusion and complexity. It is idle to hope that this vast panorama can arouse great interest in the West and even in India it is unlikely that many would now approach its gigantic recital with premonitions of delight. It is rather as a necessary background that its main outlines must be grasped, for without them Krishna's character and career can hardly be explained.

The epic begins with two rival families each possessed of a common ancestor, Kuru, but standing in bitter rivalry to each other. Kuru is succeeded by his second son, Pandu, and later by Dhritarashtra, his first son but blind. Pandu has five sons, who are called Pandavas after him, while Dhritarashtra has a hundred sons called Kauravas after Kuru their common grandfather. As children the two families grow up at the same court, but almost immediately jealousies arise which are to have a deadly outcome. Hatred begins when in boyish contests the Pandavas outdo the Kauravas. The latter resent their arrogance and presently their father, the blind king, is persuaded to approve a plot by which the five Pandavas will be killed. They are to sleep in a house which during the night will be burnt down. The plot, however, miscarries. The house is burnt, but unbeknown to the Kauravas, the five brothers escape and taking with them their mother, Kunti, go for safety to the forest. Here they wander for a while disguised as Brahmans or priests but reach at last the kingdom of Panchala. The King of Panchala has a daughter, Draupadi, whose husband is to be chosen by a public archery competition. Arjuna, one of the five brothers, wins the contest and gains her as bride. The Pandavas, however, are polyandrous and thus, on being married to one brother, Draupadi is also married to the other four. At the wedding the Pandavas disclose their identities. The Kauravas learn that they are still alive and in due course are reconciled. They reinstate the Pandavas and give them half the kingdom. Before Arjuna, however, can profit from the truce, he infringes by accident his elder brother's privacy by stumbling on him while he is with their common wife. As a consequence he violates a standing agreement and has no alternative but to go into exile for twelve years. Arjuna leaves the court, visits other lands, acquires a new wife and makes a new alliance. In other respects, all is well and the two families look forward to many years of peaceful co-existence.

The fates, however, seem determined on their destruction. The leader of the Pandavas is their eldest brother, Yudhisthira. He conquers many other lands and is encouraged to claim the title, 'ruler of the world.' The claim is made at a great sacrifice accompanied by a feast. The claim incenses the Kauravas and once again the ancient feud revives. Themselves expert gamblers, they challenge Yudhisthira to a contest by dice. Yudhisthira stupidly agrees and wagering first his kingdom, then his brothers and finally his wife, loses all and goes again into exile. With him go the other Pandavas, including Arjuna who has since returned. For twelve years they roam the forests, brooding on their fate and planning revenge. When their exile ends, they at once declare war. Both sides seek allies, efforts at peacemaking are foiled and the two clash on the battle-field of Kurukshetra. For eighteen days the battle rages till finally the Pandavas are victorious. Their success, however, is at an appalling cost. During the contest all five Pandavas lose their sons. The hundred sons of their rival, the blind king Dhritarashtra, are dead and with a sense of tragic futility, the epic ends.

It is as an actor in this tangled drama that Krishna appears. Alongside the Pandavas and the Kauravas in Northern India is a powerful people, the Yadavas. They live by grazing cattle but possess towns including a capital, the city of Dwarka in Western India. At this capital resides their ruler or king and with him is a powerful prince, Krishna. This Krishna is related to the rival families, for his father, Vasudeva, is brother of Kunti, the Pandavas' mother. From the outset, therefore, he is placed in intimate proximity to the chief protagonists. For the moment, however, he himself is not involved and it is only after the Pandavas have gone into exile and reached the kingdom of Panchala that he makes his entrance. The occasion is the archery contest for the hand of Draupadi. Krishna is there as an honoured guest and when Arjuna makes the winning shot, he immediately recognizes the five Pandavas as his kinsmen although as refugees they are still disguised as Brahmans. When the assembled princes angrily protest at Draupadi's union with a Brahman, and seem about to fight, Krishna intervenes and persuades them to accept the decision. Later he secretly meets the Pandavas and sends them wedding presents. Already, therefore, he is fulfilling a significant role. He is a powerful leader, a relative of the central figures and if only because the feud is not his own, he is above the conflict and to some extent capable of influencing its outcome.

His next appearance brings him closer still to the Pandavas. When Arjuna is exiled for his breach of marriage etiquette, he visits Krishna in his city of Dwarka. A great festival is held and in the course of it Arjuna falls in love with Krishna's sister, Subhadra. Krishna favours the marriage but advises Arjuna to marry her by capture. Arjuna does so and by becoming Krishna's brother-in-law cements still further their relationship.

This friendship has one further consequence, for, after Arjuna has completed his exile and returned to the Pandava court, Krishna visits him and the two go into the country for a picnic. 'After a few days, Arjuna said to Krishna, "The summer days have come. Let us go to the River Jumna, amuse ourselves with some friends and come back in the evening." Krishna replied, "I would like that very much. Let us go for a bathe." So Arjuna and Krishna set out with their friends. Reaching a fine spot fit for pleasure and overgrown with trees, where several tall houses had been built, the party went inside. Food and wine, wreaths of flowers and fragrant perfumes were laid out and at once they began to frolic at their will. The girls in the party with delightful rounded haunches, large breasts and handsome eyes began to flirt as Arjuna and Krishna commanded. Some played about in the woods, some in the water, some inside the houses. And Draupadi and Subhadra who were also in the party gave the girls and women costly dresses and garments. Then some of them began to dance, some to sing, some laughed and joked, some drank wine. And the houses and woods, filled with the noise of flutes and drums, became the very seat of pleasure.'[1]

A little later, Krishna is accorded special status. At the sacrifice performed by Yudhisthira as 'ruler of the world,' gifts of honour are distributed. Krishna is among the assembled guests and is proposed as first recipient. Only one person objects, a certain king Sisupala, who nurses a standing grievance against him. A quarrel ensues and during it Krishna kills him. Krishna's priority is then acclaimed but the incident serves also to demonstrate his ability as a fighter.

[1] *Mahabharata, Adi Parva*, Section 224 (Roy, I, 615-16).

One other aspect of Krishna's character remains to be noted. Besides being a bold warrior, he is above all an astute and able ally. During the Pandavas' final exile in the forest, he urges them to repudiate their banishment and make war. When the exile is over and war is near, he acts as peace-maker, urging the Kauravas to make concessions. When he is foiled by Duryodhana, the blind king's son, he attempts to have him kidnapped. Finally, once the great battle is joined, he offers both sides a choice. Each may have the help either of himself alone or of his immediate kinsmen, the Vrishnis. The Vrishnis will fight in the battle, while Krishna himself will merely advise from a distance. The Kauravas choose the fighters, the Pandavas Krishna. Krishna accordingly aids the Pandavas with counsel. He accompanies Arjuna as his charioteer and during the battle is a constant advocate of treachery. As Karna, a leading Kaurava, fights Arjuna, his chariot gets stuck and he dismounts to see to it. The rules of war demand that Arjuna should now break off but Krishna urges him to continue and Karna is killed unresisting. Similarly when Bhima, one of the five Pandava brothers, is fighting Duryodhana with his club, Krishna eggs him on to deal a foul blow. Bhima does so and Duryodhana dies from a broken thigh. In all these encounters, Krishna shows himself completely amoral, achieving his ends by the very audacity of his means.

So far, Krishna's character is merely that of a feudal magnate, and there is nothing in his views or conduct to suggest that he is Vishnu or God. Two incidents in the epic, however, suddenly reveal his true role. The first is when Yudhisthira has gambled away Draupadi and the Kauravas are intent on her dishonour. They attempt to make her naked. As one of them tries to remove her clothes, Draupadi beseeches Krishna as Vishnu to intervene and save her. Krishna does so and by his help she remains clothed however many times her dress is removed. The second occasion is on the final battle-field of Kurukshetra. Arjuna, seeing so many brothers, uncles and cousins ranged on either side is moved to pity at the senseless nature of the strife and confides his anguished doubts in Krishna. Krishna seems, at first, to be only his friend, his brother-in-law, and adviser. He points out that to a warrior nothing is nobler than a righteous war and declares, 'Do your duty always but without attachment.' He then advocates the two paths of *yoga* (knowledge) and *dharma* (righteousness). 'Even if a man falls away from the practice of *yoga*, he will still win the heaven of the doers of good deeds and dwell there many long years. After that, he will be reborn into the home of pure and prosperous parents. He will then regain that spiritual discernment which he acquired in his former body; and so he will strive harder than ever for perfection. Because of his practices in the previous life, he will be driven on toward union with the Spirit, even in spite of himself. For the man who has once asked the way to the Spirit goes farther than any mere fulfiller of the Vedic rituals. By struggling hard, that yogi will move gradually towards perfection through many births and reach the highest goal at last.'[1]

But it is the path of *bhakti* or devotion to a personal God which commands Krishna's strongest approval and leads him to make his startling revelation. 'Have your mind in Me, be devoted to Me. To Me shall you come. What is true I promise. Dear are you to Me. They who make Me their supreme object, they to Me are dear. Though I am the unborn, the changeless Self, I condition my nature and am born by my power. To save the good and destroy evildoers, to establish the right, I am born from age to age. He who knows this when he comes to die is not reborn but comes to Me.' He speaks, in fact, as Vishnu himself.

This declaration is to prove the vital clue to Krishna's character. It is to be expanded in later texts and is to account for the fervour with which he is soon to be adored. For the present, however, his claim is in the nature of an aside. After the battle, he resumes his life as a prince and it is more for his shrewdness as a councillor than his teaching as God that he is honoured and revered. Yet special majesty surrounds him and when, thirty-six years after the conflict, a hunter mistakes him for a deer and kills him by shooting him in the right foot[2], the Pandavas are inconsolable. They retreat to the Himalayas, die one by one and are translated to Indra's heaven.[3]

Such an account is obviously a great advance on the *Chandogya Upanishad*. Yet, as we ponder its intricate drama, we are faced with several intractable issues. It is true that a detailed character has emerged, a figure who is identified with definite actions and certain clear-cut principles. It is true also that his character as Vishnu has been asserted. But it is Krishna the feudal hero who throughout the story takes, by far, the leading part. Between this hero and Krishna the God, there is no very clear connection. The circumstances in which Vishnu has taken form as Krishna are nowhere made plain. Except on the two occasions mentioned, Krishna is apparently not recognized as God by others and does not himself claim this status. Indeed it is virtually only as an afterthought that the epic is used to

[1] C. Isherwood and S. Prabhavananda, *The Song of God, Bhagavad-Gita*, 86–7.
[2] Plate 2. [3] Note 5.

transmit his great sermon, and almost by accident that he becomes the most significant figure in the story. Even the sermon at first sight seems at variance with his actions as a councillor—his repeated recourse to treachery ill consorting with the paramountcy of duty. In point of fact, such a conflict can be easily reconciled for if God is supreme, he is above and beyond morals. He can act in any way he pleases and yet, as God, can expect and receive the highest reverence. God, in fact, is superior to ethics. And this viewpoint is, in fact, to prove a basic assumption in later versions of the story. Here it is sufficient to note that while the *Mahabharata* describes these two contrasting modes of behaviour, no attempt is made to face the exact issue. Krishna as God has been introduced rather than explained and we are left with the feeling that much more than has been recorded remains to be said.

This feeling may well have dogged the writers who put the *Mahabharata* into its present shape for, a little later, possibly during the sixth century A.D., an appendix was added. This appendix was called the *Harivansa* or Genealogy of Krishna[1] and in it were provided all those details so manifestly wanting in the epic itself. The exact nature of Krishna is explained—the circumstances of his birth, his youth and childhood, the whole being welded into a coherent scheme. In this story Krishna the feudal magnate takes a natural place but there is no longer any contradiction between his character as a prince and his character as God. He is, above all, an incarnation of Vishnu and his immediate purpose is to vanquish a particular tyrant and hearten the righteous. This viewpoint is maintained in the *Vishnu Purana*, another text of about the sixth century and is developed and illustrated in the tenth and eleventh books of the *Bhagavata Purana*. It is this latter text—a vast compendium of perhaps the ninth or tenth century—which affords the fullest account in literature of Krishna's story.

[1] Note 6.

III

THE *BHAGAVATA PURANA:* THE COWHERD

(*i*) *Birth and Early Adventures*

The *Bhagavata Purana* is couched in the form of a dialogue between a sage and a king. The king is the successor of the Pandavas but is doomed to die within a week for having by accident insulted a holy ascetic. To ensure his salvation, he spends the week listening to the *Bhagavata Purana* and concentrating his mind on Krishna whom he declares to be his helper.[1]

Book Ten begins by describing the particular situation which leads to Krishna's birth. The scene is Mathura, a town in northern India, adjoining the kingdom of the Kauravas. The surrounding country is known as Braj and its ruling families are the Yadavas. Just outside Mathura is the district of Gokula which is inhabited by cowherds. These are on friendly terms with the Yadavas, but are inferior to them in caste and status. The time is some fifty years or more before the battle of Kurukshetra and the ruling king is Ugrasena. Ugrasena's queen is Pavanarekha and a mishap to her sets in train a series of momentous events.

One day she is taking the air in a park, when she misses her way and finds herself alone. A demon, Drumalika, is passing and, entranced by her grace, decides to ravish her. He takes the form of her husband, Ugrasena, and despite Pavanarekha's protests proceeds to enjoy her. Afterwards he assumes his true shape. Pavanarekha is dismayed but the demon tells her that he has given her a son who will 'vanquish the nine divisions of the earth, rule supreme and fight Krishna.' Pavanarekha tells her maids that a monkey has been troubling her. Ten months later a son is born. He is named Kansa and the court rejoices.

As Kansa grows up he reveals his demon's nature. He ignores his father's words, murders children and defeats in battle King Jarasandha of Magadha.[2] The latter gives him two daughters in marriage. He then deposes his father, throws him into prison, assumes his powers and bans the worship of Vishnu. As his crimes increase, he

---

[1] Note 7.
[2] Magadha—a region corresponding to present-day South Bihar.

extends his conquests. At last Earth can bear the burden no longer and appeals to the gods to approach the supreme Deity, Brahma, to rid her of the load. Brahma as Creator can hardly do this, but Vishnu as Preserver agrees to intervene and plans are laid. Among the Yadava nobility are two upright persons. The first is Devaka, the younger brother of King Ugrasena and thus an uncle to the tyrant. The second is a certain Vasudeva. Devaka has six daughters, all of whom he marries to Vasudeva. The seventh is called Devaki. Vishnu announces that Devaki will also be married to Vasudeva, and plucking out two of his hairs—one black and one white—he declares that these will be the means by which he will ease Earth's burden. The white hair is part of Sesha, the great serpent, which is itself a part of Vishnu. and this will be impersonated as Devaki's seventh child. The black hair is Vishnu's own self which will be impersonated as Devaki's eighth child. The child from the white hair will be known as Balarama and the child from the black hair as Krishna. As Krishna, Vishnu will then kill Kansa. Earth is gratified and retires and the stage is set for Krishna's coming.

Devaki, with Kansa's approval, is now married to Vasudeva. The wedding is being celebrated in the grandest manner when a voice from heaven is heard saying, 'Kansa, the eighth son of her whom you are now escorting will cause your destruction. You shall die at his hand.' Kansa is greatly alarmed and is about to slay Devaki when Vasudeva agrees to yield him all their sons. Kansa accordingly spares her. Each of Devaki's first six sons, however, is delivered up at birth and each is slaughtered.

As the time for fulfilling the prophecy approaches, Kansa grows fearful. He learns that gods and goddesses are being born as cowherds and cowgirls and, interpreting this as a sign that Krishna's birth is near, he commands his men to slaughter every cowherd in the city. A great round-up ensues and many cowherds are killed. The leading cowherd is a wealthy herdsman named Nanda, who lives with his wife Yasoda in the country district of Gokula. Although of lower caste, he is Vasudeva's chief friend and in view of the imminent dangers confronting his family, it is to Nanda that Vasudeva now sends one of his other wives, Rohini. Devaki has meanwhile conceived her seventh son, the white hair of Vishnu, and soon to be recognized as Krishna's brother. To avoid his murder by Kansa, Vishnu has the foetus transferred from Devaki's womb to that of Rohini, and the child, named Balarama, is born to Rohini, Kansa being informed that Devaki has miscarried. The eighth pregnancy now occurs. Kansa increases his precautions. Devaki and

Vasudeva are handcuffed and manacled. Guards are mounted and besides these, elephants, lions and dogs are placed outside. The unborn child, however, tells them not to fear and Devaki and Vasudeva compose their minds.

Krishna is now born, dark as a cloud and with eyes like lotuses. He is clad in a yellow vest and wears a crown. He takes the form of Vishnu and commands Vasudeva to bear him to Nanda's house in Gokula and substitute him for the infant daughter who has just been born to Yasoda, Nanda's wife. Devaki and Vasudeva worship him. The vision then fades and they discover the new-born child crying at their side. They debate what to do—Devaki urging Vasudeva to take the baby to Nanda's house where Rohini, his other wife, is still living and where Yasoda will receive it. Vasudeva is wondering how to escape when his handcuffs and chains fall off, the doors open and the guards are seen to be asleep. Placing Krishna in a basket, he puts it on his head and sets out for Gokula. As he goes, lions roar, the rain pours down and the river Jumna faces him. There is no help but to ford it and Vasudeva accordingly enters the stream. The water gets higher and higher until it reaches his nose. When he can go no farther, the infant Krishna stretches out a foot, calms the river and the water subsides. Vasudeva now arrives at Nanda's house where he finds that Yasoda has borne a girl and is in a trance. Vasudeva puts Krishna beside her, takes up the baby girl, recrosses the river and joins Devaki in her prison. The doors shut, the handcuffs and fetters close on them again and as the baby starts to cry, the guards awake. A sentry then carries Kansa the news. Kansa hurries to the spot, seizes the child and tries to dash it on a stone. As he does so the child becomes the goddess Devi and exclaiming that Kansa's enemy is born elsewhere and nothing can save him, vanishes into heaven.[1] Kansa is greatly shaken and orders all male children to be killed,[2] but releases Vasudeva and Devaki.

Meanwhile Nanda, the rich herdsman, is celebrating the birth. Pandits and astrologers are sent for, the child's horoscope is cast and his destiny foretold. He will be a second deity like Brahma himself. He will destroy demons, relieve the land of Braj of all its cares, be called the lord of the cowgirls and be praised the whole world over. Nanda promises to dedicate cows, loads the Brahmans with presents, and summons all the musicians and singers of the city. Singing, dancing and music break forth, the courtyards throng with people, and the cowherds of Gokula come in with their wives. On their heads are pitchers full of curd and as a magical means of ensuring

[1] Plate 3. [2] Note 8.

prosperity, they proceed to throw it over the gathering. Nanda presents them with cloth and betel and they depart elated at the news.

Some days later Nanda learns of Kansa's order to seize all male children and, deeming it prudent to offer presents, he collects the cowherds in a body and goes to Mathura to pay tribute. Kansa receives him and on his way back Vasudeva meets him at the river. He dare not disclose his secret that Krishna is not Nanda's son but his own. At the same time he cannot suppress his anxiety as a father. He contents himself by telling Nanda that demons and evil spirits are abroad seeking to destroy young children and urges him to return to Gokula as quickly as possible.

The *Purana* now concentrates on two main themes: on Krishna's infancy in Gokula, dilating on his baby pranks, his capacity for mischief, the love he arouses in the hearts of his foster-mother, Yasoda, and of all the married cowgirls and, secondly, on his supernatural powers and skill in ridding the country of troublesome demons. These are at first shown as hostile to Krishna only, but as the story unfolds, his role gradually widens and we see him acting as the cowherds' ally, protecting them from harm, attacking the forces of evil and thus fulfilling the supreme purpose for which he has been born. From time to time the cowherds realize that Krishna is Vishnu and adore him as God. Then amnesia intervenes. They retain no recollection of the vision and see him simply as a youthful cowherd, charming in manner, whose skill in slaying demons arouses their love. In this way Krishna lives among them—in fact, God, but in the eyes of the people, a young boy.[1]

The first demon to threaten Krishna's life is a huge ogress named Putana. Her role is that of child-killer—any child who is suckled in the night by Putana instantly dying. Putana assumes the form of a sweet and charming girl, dabs her breasts with poison and while Nanda is still at Mathura, comes gaily to his house. Entranced by her appearance, Yasoda allows her to hold the baby Krishna and then to suckle him. Krishna, however, is impervious to the poison, and fastening his mouth to her breast, he begins to suck her life out with the milk. Putana, feeling her life going, rushes wildly from the village, but to no avail. Krishna continues sucking and the ogress dies. When Yasoda and Rohini catch up with her, they find her huge carcass lying on the ground with Krishna still sucking her breast. 'Taking him up quickly and kissing him, they pressed him to their bosoms and hurried home.'

[1] Note 9.

Nanda now arrives from Mathura and congratulates the cowherds on their escape—so great was Putana's size that her body might have crushed and overwhelmed the whole colony. He then arranges for her burning but as her flesh is being consumed, a strange perfume is noticed for Krishna, when killing her, had granted her salvation.

A second demon now intervenes. It is twenty-seven days since Krishna's birth. Brahmans and cowherds have been summoned to a feast, the cowgirls are singing songs and everyone is laughing and eating. Krishna for the time being is out of their minds, having been put to sleep beneath a heavy cart loaded with pitchers. A little later he wakes up, begins to cry for the breast and finding no one there wriggles about and starts to suck a toe. At this moment the demon, Saktasura, is flying through the sky. He notices the child and alights on the cart. His weight cracks it but before the cart can collapse, Krishna kicks out so sharply that the demon dies and the cart falls to pieces. Hearing a great crash, the cowgirls dash to the spot, marvelling that although the cart is in splinters and all the pots broken, Krishna has survived.

The third attack occurs when Krishna is five months old. Yasoda is sitting with him in her lap when she notices that he has suddenly become very heavy. At the same time, the whirlwind demon, Trinavarta, raises a great storm. The sky darkens, trees are uprooted and thatch dislodged. As Yasoda sets Krishna down, Trinavarta seizes him and whirls him into the air. Yasoda finds him suddenly gone and calls out, 'Krishna, Krishna.' The cowgirls and cowherds join her in the search, peering for him in the gusty gloom of the dark storm. Full of misery, they search the forest and can find him nowhere. Krishna, riding through the air, however, can see their distress. He twists Trinavarta round, forces him down and dashes him to death against a stone. As he does so, the storm lightens, the wind drops and the cowherds and cowgirls regain their homes. There they discover a demon lying dead with Krishna playing on its chest. Filled with relief, Yasoda picks him up and hugs him to her breast.

Vasudeva now instructs his family priest, Garga the sage, to go to Gokula, meet Nanda and give Krishna and Balarama proper names. Rohini, he points out, has had a son, Balarama, and Nanda has also had a son, Krishna. It is time that each should be formally named. The sage is delighted to receive the commission and on arriving is warmly welcomed. He declines, however, to announce the children's names in public, fearing that his connection with Vasudeva will cause Raja Kansa to connect Krishna with the eighth child—his fated enemy. Nanda accordingly takes him inside his house and there the sage names the two children. Balarama is given seven names, but Krishna's names, he declares, are numberless. Since, however, Krishna was once born in Vasudeva's house, he is called Vasudeva. As to their qualities, the sage goes on, both are gods. It is impossible to understand their state, but having killed Kansa, they will remove the burdens of the world. He then goes silently away. This is the first time that Nanda and Yasoda are told the true facts of Krishna's birth. They do not, however, make any comment and for the time being it is as if they are still quite ignorant of Krishna's destiny. They continue to treat him as their son and no hint escapes them of his true identity.

Meanwhile Krishna, along with Rohini's son, Balarama, is growing up as a baby. He crawls about the courtyard, lisps his words, plays with toys and pulls the calves' tails, Yasoda and Rohini all the time showering upon him their doting love. When he can walk, Krishna starts to go about with other children and there then ensues a series of naughty pranks. His favourite pastime is to raid the houses of the cowgirls, pilfer their cream and curds, steal butter and upset milk pails. When, as sometimes happens, the butter is hung from the roof, they pile up some of the household furniture. One of the boys then mounts upon it, another climbs on his shoulders, and in this way gets the butter down.[1] As the pilfering increases, the married cowgirls learn that Krishna is the ringleader and contrive one day to catch him in the act. 'You little thief,' they say, 'At last we've caught you. So it's you who took our butter and curds. You won't escape us now.' And taking him by the hand they march him to Yasoda. Krishna, however, is not to be outwitted. Employing his supernatural powers, he substitutes the cowgirls' own sons for himself and while they go to Yasoda, himself slips off and joins his playmates in the fields. When the cowgirls reach Yasoda, they complain of Krishna's thefts and tell her that at last they have caught him and here he is. Yasoda answers, 'But this is not Krishna. These are your own sons.' The cowgirls look at the children, discover the trick, are covered in confusion and burst out laughing. Yasoda then sends for Krishna and forbids him to steal from other people's houses. Krishna pretends to be highly indignant. He calls the cowgirls liars and accuses them of always making him do their work. If he is not having to hold a milk pail or a calf, he says, he is doing a household chore or even keeping watch for them while they neglect

[1] Plate 4.

their work and gossip. The cowgirls listen in astonishment and go away.

Another day Krishna is playing in a courtyard and takes it into his head to eat some dirt. Yasoda is told of it and in a fit of anger runs towards him with a stick. 'Why are you eating mud?' she cries. 'What mud?' says Krishna. 'The mud one of your friends has just told me you have eaten. If you haven't eaten it, open your mouth.' Krishna opens it and looking inside, Yasoda sees the three worlds. In a moment of perception, she realizes that Krishna is God. 'What am I doing in looking upon the Lord of the three worlds as my son?' she cries. Then the vision fades and she picks up Krishna and kisses him.

Another day, Yasoda asks the married cowgirls to assist her in churning milk. They clean the house, set up a large vessel, prepare the churning staff and string, and start to churn. Krishna is awakened by the noise and finding no one about comes crying to Yasoda. 'I am hungry, mother,' he says. 'Why have you not given me anything to eat?' And in a fit of petulance he starts to throw the butter about and kick over the pitchers. Yasoda tells him not to be so naughty, sits him on her lap and gives him some milk. While she is doing this, a cowgirl tells her that the milk has boiled over and Yasoda jumps up leaving Krishna alone. While she is away he breaks the pots, scatters the curds, makes a mess of all the rooms and, taking a pot full of butter, runs away with it into the fields. There he seats himself on an upturned mortar, assembles the other boys and vastly pleased with himself, laughingly shares the butter out. When Yasoda returns and sees the mess, she seizes a stick and goes to look for Krishna. She cannot find it in her heart, however, to be angry for long and when Krishna says, 'Mother, let me go. I did not do it,' she laughs and throws the stick away. Then pretending to be still very angry, she takes him home and ties him to a mortar. A little later a great crash is heard. Two huge trees have fallen and when the cowherds hurry to the spot, they find that Krishna has dragged the mortar between the trunks, pulled them down and is quietly sitting between them.[1] Two youths—by name Nala and Kuvara—have been imprisoned in the trees and Krishna's action has released them. When she sees that Krishna is safe, Yasoda unties him from the mortar and hugs him to her.

This incident of the trees now forces Nanda to make a decision. The various happenings have been profoundly unnerving and he feels that it is no longer safe to stay in Gokula. He decides therefore

[1] Plate 5.

to move a day's march farther on, to cross the river and settle in the forests of Brindaban. The cowherds accordingly load up their possessions on carts and the move ensues.[1]

The story now enters its second phase. Krishna is no longer a mischievous baby, indulging in tantrums yet wringing the heart with his childish antics. He is now five years old and of an age to make himself useful. He asks to be allowed to graze the calves. At first Yasoda is unwilling. 'We have got so many servants,' she says. 'It is their job to take the calves out. Why go yourself? You are the protection of my eye-lids and dearer to me than my eyes.' Krishna, however, insists and in the end she entrusts him and Balarama to the other young cowherds, telling them on no account to leave them alone in the forest, but to bring them safely home. Her words are, in fact, only too necessary, for Kansa, the tyrant king, is still in quest of the child who is to kill him. His demon minions are still on the alert, attacking any likely boy, and as Krishna plays with the cowherds and tends the calves, he suffers a further series of attacks.

A cow demon, Vatsasura, tries to mingle with the herd. The calves sense its presence and as it sidles up, Krishna seizes it by the hind leg, whirls it round his head and dashes it to death. A crane demon, Bakasura, then approaches. The cowherds recognize it, but while they are wondering how to escape, the crane opens its beak and engulfs Krishna. Krishna, however, becomes so hot that the crane cannot retain him. It lets him go. Krishna then tears its beak in two, rounds up the calves and taking the cowherd boys with him, returns home.

Another day Krishna is out in the forest with the cowherds and the calves, when a snake demon, Ugrasura, sucks them into its mouth. Krishna expands his body to such an extent that the snake bursts. The calves and cowherd children come tumbling out and all praise Krishna for saving them. On the way back, Krishna suggests that they should have a picnic and choosing a great *kadam* tree, they sweep the place clean, set out their food and proceed to enjoy it. As they eat, the gods look down, noting how handsome the young Krishna has grown. Among the gods is Brahma, who decides to tease Krishna by hiding the calves while the cowherd children are eating.[2] He takes them to a cave and when Krishna goes in search of them, hides the cowherd children as well. Krishna, however, is not to be deterred. Creating duplicates of every calf and boy he brings them home. No one detects that anything is wrong and for a year

[1] Plate 6. In the *Harivansa*, the cause of the migration is given as a dangerous influx of wolves.   [2] Note 10.

they live as if nothing has happened. Brahma has meanwhile sunk himself in meditation, but suddenly recalls his prank and hurries out to set matters right. He is astonished to find the original calves and children still sleeping in the cave, while their counterparts roam the forest. He humbly worships Krishna, restores the original calves and children and returns to his abode. When the cowherd children awake, Krishna shows them the calves. No one realizes what has happened. The picnic continues and laughing and playing they go home.

We now enter the third phase of Krishna's childhood. He is eight years old and is therefore competent to graze not merely the calves but the cows as well.[1] Nanda accordingly performs the necessary ritual and Krishna goes with the cowherds to the forest.

An idyllic phase in Krishna's life now starts. 'At this time Krishna and Balarama, accompanied by the cow-boys, traversed the forests, that echoed with the hum of bees and the peacock's cry. Sometimes they sang in chorus or danced together; sometimes they sought shelter from the cold beneath the trees; sometimes they decorated themselves with flowery garlands, sometimes with peacocks' feathers; sometimes they stained themselves of various hues with the minerals of the mountain; sometimes weary they reposed on beds of leaves, and sometimes imitated in mirth the muttering of the thundercloud; sometimes they excited their juvenile associates to sing, and sometimes they mimicked the cry of the peacock with their pipes. In this manner participating in various feelings and emotions, and affectionately attached to each other, they wandered, sporting and happy, through the wood. At eveningtide came Krishna and Balarama, like to cowboys, along with the cows and the cowherds. At eveningtide the two immortals, having come to the cow-pens, joined heartily in whatever sports amused the sons of the herdsmen.'[2]

One day as they are grazing the cows, they play a game. Krishna divides the cows and cowherds into two sides and collecting flowers and fruits pretends that they are weapons. They then stage a mock battle, pelting each other with the fruits. A little later Balarama takes them to a grove of palm trees. The ass demon, Dhenuka, guards it. Balarama, however, seizes it by its hind legs, twists it round and hurls it into a high tree. From the tree the demon falls down dead. When Dhenuka's companion asses hasten to the spot, Krishna kills them also. The cowherds then pick the coconuts to their hearts' content, fill a quantity of baskets and having grazed the cows, go strolling home.

[1] Plate 7.   [2] Note 7.

The next morning Krishna rises early, calls the cowherds and takes the cows to the forest. As they are grazing them by the Jumna, they reach a dangerous whirlpool. In this whirlpool lives the giant snake, Kaliya, whose poison has befouled the water, curdling it into a great froth. The cowherds and the cattle drink some of it, are taken ill, but revive at Krishna's glance. They then play ball. A solitary *kadam* tree is on the bank. Krishna climbs it and a cowherd throws the ball up to him. The ball goes into the water and Krishna, thinking this the moment for quelling the great snake, plunges in after it. Kaliya detects that an intruder has entered the pool, begins to spout poison and fire and encircles Krishna in its coils. In their alarm the cowherds send word to Nanda and along with Yasoda, Rohini and the other cowgirls, he hastens to the scene. Krishna can no longer be seen and in her agitation Yasoda is about to throw herself in. Krishna, however, is merely playing with the snake. In a moment he expands his body, jumps from the coils and begins to dance on the snake's heads. 'Having the weight of three worlds,' the *Purana* says, 'Krishna was very heavy.' The snake fails to sustain this dancing burden, its heads droop and blood flows from its tongues. It is about to die when the snake-queens bow at Krishna's feet and implore his mercy. Krishna relents, spares the snake's life but banishes it to a distant island.[1] He then leaves the river, but the exhaustion of the cowherds and cowgirls is so great that they decide to stay in the forest for the night and return to Brindaban next morning. Their trials, however, are far from over. At midnight there is a heavy storm and a huge conflagration. Scarlet flames leap up, dense smoke engulfs the forest and many cattle are burnt alive. Finding themselves in great danger, Nanda, Yasoda and the cowherds call on Krishna to save them. Krishna quietly rises up, sucks the fire into his mouth and ends the blaze.

The hot weather now comes. Trees are heavy with blossom, peacocks strut in the glades and a general lethargy seizes the cowherds. One day Krishna and his friends are out with the cattle when Pralamba, a demon in human form, comes to join them. Krishna warns Balarama of the demon's presence and tells him to await an opportunity to kill him. He then divides the cowherds into two groups and starts them on the game of guessing fruits and flowers. Krishna's side loses and as a penalty they have to run a certain distance carrying Balarama's side on their shoulders. Pralamba carries Balarama. He runs so fast that he quickly outstrips the others. As he reaches the forest, he changes size, becoming 'large as

[1] Plate 8.

a black hill.' He is about to kill Balarama when Balarama himself rains blows upon him and kills him instead.[1] While this is happening, the cows get lost, another forest fire ensues and Krishna has once again to intervene. He extinguishes the fire, regains the cattle and escorts the cowherds to their homes.[2] When the others hear what has happened, they are filled with wonder 'but obtain no clue to the actions of Krishna.'

During all this time, Krishna as 'son' of the wealthiest and most influential cowherd, Nanda, has been readily accepted by the cowherd children as their natural leader. His lack of fear, his bravery in coping with demons, his resourcefulness in extricating the cowherds from awkward situations, his complete self-confidence and finally his princely bearing have revealed him as someone altogether above the ordinary. From time to time he has disclosed his true nature as Vishnu but almost immediately has exercised his 'illusory' power and prevented the cowherds from remembering it. He has consequently lived among them as God but their love and admiration are still for him as a boy. It is at this point that the *Purana* now moves to what is perhaps its most significant phase—a description of Krishna's effects on the cowgirls.

(ii) *The Loves of the Cowgirls*

We have seen how during his infancy Krishna's pranks have already made him the darling of the women. As he grows up, he acquires a more adult charm. In years he is still a boy but we are suddenly confronted with what is to prove the very heart of the story—his romances with the cowgirls. Although all of them are married, the cowgirls find his presence irresistible and despite the warnings of morality and the existence of their husbands, each falls utterly in love with him. As Krishna wanders in the forest, the cowgirls can talk of nothing but his charms. They do their work but their thoughts are on him. They stay at home but all the time each is filled with desperate longing. One day Krishna plays on his flute in the forest. Playing the flute is the cowherds' special art and Krishna has, therefore, learnt it in his childhood. But, as in everything else, his skill is quite exceptional and Krishna's playing has thus a beauty all its own. From where they are working the cowgirls hear it and at once are plunged in agitation. They gather on the road and say to each other, 'Krishna is dancing and singing in the forest and will not be home till evening. Only then shall we see him and be happy.'

[1] Plate 9.   [2] Plate 10.

One cowgirl says, 'That happy flute to be played on by Krishna! Little wonder that having drunk the nectar of his lips the flute should trill like the clouds. Alas! Krishna's flute is dearer to him than we are for he keeps it with him night and day. The flute is our rival. Never is Krishna parted from it.' A second cowgirl speaks. 'It is because the flute continually thought of Krishna that it gained this bliss.' And a third says, 'Oh! why has Krishna not made us into flutes that we might stay with him day and night?' The situation in fact has changed overnight for far from merely appealing to the cowgirls' maternal instincts, Krishna is now the darling object of their most intense passion.

Faced with this situation, the cowgirls discuss how best to gain Krishna as their lover. They recall that bathing in the early winter is believed to wipe out sin and fulfil the heart's desires. They accordingly go to the river Jumna, bathe in its waters and after making clay images of Parvati, Siva's consort, pray to her to make Krishna theirs. They go on doing this for many days.

One day they choose a part of the river where there is a steep bank. Taking off their clothes they leave them on the grass verge, enter the water and swim around calling out their love for Krishna. Unknown to them, Krishna is in the vicinity and is grazing the cows. He steals quietly up, sees them in the river, makes their clothes into a bundle and then climbs up with it into a tree. When the cowgirls come out of the water, they cannot find their clothes until at last one of them spies Krishna sitting in the tree. The cowgirls hurriedly squat down in the water entreating Krishna to return their clothes. Krishna, however, tells them to come up out of the water and ask him one by one. The cowgirls say, 'But this will make us naked. You are making an end of our friendship.' Krishna says, 'Then you shall not have your clothes back.' The cowgirls answer, 'Why do you treat us so? It is only for you that we have bathed all these days.' Krishna answers, 'If that is really so, then do not be bashful or deceive me. Come and take your clothes.' Finding no alternative, the cowgirls argue amongst themselves that since Krishna already knows the secrets of their minds and bodies, there is no point in being ashamed before him, and they come up out of the water shielding their nakedness with their hands.[1] Krishna tells them to raise their hands and then he will return their clothes. The cowgirls do so begging him not to make fun of them and to give them at least something in return. Krishna now hands the clothes back giving as excuse for his conduct the following somewhat specious

[1] Plate 11.

reason. 'I was only giving you a lesson,' he says. 'The god Varuna lives in water, so if anyone goes naked into it he loses his character. This was a secret, but now you know it.' Then he relents. 'I have told you this because of your love. Go home now but come back in the early autumn and we will dance together.' Hearing this the cowgirls put on their clothes and wild with love return to their village.

At this point the cowgirls' love for Krishna is clearly physical. Although precocious in his handling of the situation, Krishna is still the rich herdsman's handsome son and it is as this rather than as God that they regard him. Yet the position is never wholly free from doubt for in loving Krishna as a youth, it is as if they are from time to time aware of adoring him as God. No precise identifications are made and yet so strong are their passions that seemingly only God himself could evoke them. And although no definite explanation is offered, it is perhaps this same idea which underlies the following incident.

One day Krishna is in the forest when his cowherd companions complain of feeling hungry. Krishna observes smoke rising from the direction of Mathura and infers that the Brahmans are cooking food preparatory to making sacrifice. He asks the cowherds to tell them that Krishna is hungry and would like some of this food. The Brahmans of Mathura angrily spurn the request, saying 'Who but a low cowherd would ask for food in the midst of a sacrifice?' 'Go and ask their wives,' Krishna says, 'for being kind and virtuous they will surely give you some.' Krishna's power with women is then demonstrated once more. His fame as a stealer of hearts has preceded him and the cowherds have only to mention his name for the wives of the Brahmans to run to serve him. They bring out gold dishes, load them with food, brush their husbands aside and hurry to the forest. One husband stops his wife, but rather than be left behind the woman leaves her body and reaches Krishna before the others. When the women arrive they marvel at Krishna's beauty. 'He is Nanda's son,' they say. 'We heard his name and everything else was driven from our minds. Let us gaze on this darling object of our lives. O Krishna, it is due to you that we have seen you and thus got rid of all our sins. Those stupid Brahmans, our husbands, mistook you for a mere man. But you are God. As God they offer to you prayers, penance, sacrifice and love. How then can they deny you food?' Krishna replies that they should not worship him for he is only the child of the cowherd, Nanda. He was hungry and they took pity on him, and he only regrets that being far from home he cannot return their hospitality. They must now go home as their presence is needed for the sacrifices and their husbands must still be waiting. So cool an answer dismays the women and they say, 'Great king, we loved your lotus-like face. We came to you despite our families. They tried to stop us but we ignored them. If they do not take us back, where shall we go? And one of us, prevented by her husband, gave her life rather than not see you.' At this Krishna smiles, reveals the woman and says, 'Whoever loves God never dies. She was here before you.' Krishna then eats the food and assuring them that their husbands will say nothing, sends them back to Mathura. When they arrive, they find the Brahmans chastened and contrite—cursing their folly in having failed to recognize Krishna as God and envious of their wives for having seen him and given him food.

Having humbled the Brahmans, Krishna now turns to the gods, choosing Indra, their chief, for attack. The moment is his annual worship when the cowherds offer sweets, rice, saffron, sandal and incense. Seeing them busy, Krishna asks Nanda what is the point of all their preparations. What good can Indra really do? he asks. He is only a god, not God himself. He is often worsted by demons and abjectly put to flight. In fact he has no power at all. Men prosper because of their virtues or their fates, not because of Indra. As cowherds, their business is to carry on agriculture and trade and to tend cows and Brahmans. Their earliest books, the Vedas, require them not to abandon their family customs and Krishna then cites as an ancient practice the custom of placating the spirits of the forests and hills. This custom, he says, they have wrongly superseded in favour of Indra and they must now revive it. Nanda sees the force of Krishna's remarks and holds a meeting. 'Do not brush aside his words as those of a mere boy,' he says. 'If we face the facts, we have really nothing to do with the ruler of the gods. It is on the forests, rivers and the great hill, Govardhana, that we really depend.' The cowherds applaud this advice, resolve to abandon the gods and in their place to worship the mountain, Govardhana. The worship of the hill is then performed. Krishna advises the cowherds to shut their eyes and the spirit of the hill will then show itself. He then assumes the spirit's form himself, telling Nanda and the cowherds that in response to their worship the mountain spirit has appeared. The cowherds' eyes are easily deceived. Beholding, as they think, Govardhana himself, they make offerings and go rejoicing home.

Such an act of defiance greatly enrages Indra and he assembles all the gods. He forgets that earlier in the story it was the gods themselves who begged Vishnu to be born on earth and that many of their number have even taken birth as cowherds and cowgirls in order to delight in Krishna as his incarnation. Instead he sees Krishna as 'a great talker, a silly unintelligent child and very proud.' He scoffs at the cowherds for regarding Krishna as a god, and in order to reinstate himself he orders the clouds to rain down torrents. The cowherds, faced with floods on every side, appeal to Krishna. Krishna, however, is fully alive to the position. He calms their fears and raising the hill Govardhana, supports it on his little finger.[1] The cowherds and cattle take shelter under it and although Indra himself comes and pours down rain for seven days, Braj and its inhabitants stay dry. Indra is compelled to admit that Vishnu has indeed descended in the form of Krishna and retires to his abode. Krishna then sets the hill down in its former place. Following this discomfiture, Indra comes down from the sky accompanied by his white elephant and by Surabhi, the cow of plenty. He offers his submission to Krishna, is pardoned and returns.

All these events bring to a head the problem which has been exercising the cowherds for long—who and what is Krishna? Obviously no simple boy could lift the mountain on his finger. He must clearly be someone much greater and they conclude that Krishna can only be Vishnu himself. They accordingly beseech him to show them the paradise of Vishnu. Krishna agrees, creates a paradise and shows it to them. The cowherds see it and praise his name. Yet it is part of the story that these flashes of insight should be evanescent—that having realized one instant that Krishna is God, the cowherds should regard him the next instant as one of themselves. Having revealed his true nature, therefore, Krishna becomes a cowherd once again and is accepted by the cowherds as being only that.

One further incident must be recorded. In compliance with a vow, Nanda assembles the cowherds and cowgirls and goes to the shrine of Devi, the Earth Mother, to celebrate Krishna's twelfth birthday. There they make lavish offerings of milk, curds and butter and thank the goddess for protecting Krishna for so long. Night comes on and they camp near the shrine. As Nanda is sleeping, a huge python begins to swallow his foot.[2] Nanda calls to Krishna, who hastens to his rescue. Logs are taken from a fire, but as soon as the snake is touched by Krishna, a handsome young man emerges and stands before him with folded hands. He explains that he was once the celestial dancer, Sudarsana who in excess of pride drove his chariot backwards and forwards a hundred times over the place

[1] Plate 12.   [2] Note 11.

where a holy man was meditating. As a consequence he was cursed and told to become a python until Krishna came and released him. To attract Krishna's attention he has seized the foot of Nanda. Krishna bids him go and, ascending his chariot, Sudarsana returns to the gods.

The *Purana* now returns to Krishna's encounters with the cowgirls, their passionate longings and ardent desire to have him as their lover. Since the incident at the river, they have been waiting for him to keep his promise. Krishna, however, has appeared blandly indifferent—going to the forest, playing with the cowherds but coldly ignoring the cowgirls themselves. When autumn comes, however, the beauty of the nights stirs his feelings. Belatedly he recalls his promise and decides to fulfil it. That night his flute sounds in the forest, its notes reaching the ears of the cowgirls and thrilling them to the core. Like girls in tribal India today, they know it is a call to love. They put on new clothes, brush aside their husbands, ignore the other members of their families and hurry to the forest. As they arrive, Krishna stands superbly before them. He wears a crown of peacocks' feathers and a yellow dhoti and his blue-black skin shines in the moonlight. As the cowgirls throng to see him, he twits them on their conduct. Are they not frightened at coming into the dark forest? What are they doing abandoning their families? Is not such wild behaviour quite unbefitting married girls? Should not a married girl obey her husband in all things and never for a moment leave him? Having enjoyed the deep forest and the moonlight, let them return at once and soothe their injured spouses. The cowgirls are stunned to hear such words, hang their heads, sigh and dig their toes into the ground. They begin to weep and at last turn on Krishna, saying 'Oh! why have you deceived us so? It was your flute that made us come. We have left our husbands for you. We live for your love. Where are we to go?' 'If you really love me,' Krishna answers 'Dance and sing with me.' His words fill the cowgirls with delight and surrounding Krishna 'like golden creepers growing on a dark-coloured hill,' they go with him to the banks of the Jumna. Here Krishna has conjured up a golden circular terrace ornamented with pearls and diamonds and cooled by sprouting plantains. The moon pours down, saturating the forest. The cowgirls' joy increases. They beautify their bodies and then, wild with love, join with Krishna in singing and dancing. Modesty deserts them and they do whatever pleases them, regarding Krishna as their lover. As the night goes on, Krishna 'appears as beautiful as the moon amidst the stars.'

As the cowgirls' ecstasies proceed, Krishna feels that they are fast exceeding themselves. They think that he is in their power and are already swelling with pride. He decides therefore to leave them suddenly, and taking a single girl with him vanishes from the dance.[1] When they find him gone, the cowgirls are at a loss to know what to do. 'Only a moment ago,' one of them says, 'Krishna's arms were about my neck, and now he has gone.' They begin to comb the forest, anxiously asking the trees, birds and animals, for news. As they go, they recall Krishna's many winning ways, his sweetnesses of character, his heart-provoking charms and begin to mimic his acts—the slaying of Putana, the quelling of Kaliya, the lifting of the hill Govardhana. One girl imitates Krishna dancing and another Krishna playing. In all these ways they strive to evoke his passionately-desired presence. At length they discover Krishna's footprints and a little farther on those of a woman beside them. They follow the trail which leads them to a bed of leaves and on the leaves they find a looking-glass. 'What was Krishna doing with this?' they ask. 'He must have taken it with him,' a cowgirl answers, 'so that while he braided his darling's hair, she could still perceive his lovely form.' And burning with love, they continue looking.

While they are searching, the particular cowgirl who has gone with Krishna is tempted to take liberties. Thinking Krishna is her slave, she complains of feeling tired and asks him to carry her on his shoulders. Krishna smiles, sits down and asks her to mount. But as she puts out her hands, he vanishes and she remains standing with hands outstretched.[2] Tears stream from her eyes. She is filled with bitter grief and cries 'O Krishna! best of lovers, where have you gone? Take pity.'

As she is bemoaning her fate, her companions arrive.[3] They put their arms around her, comfort her as best they can, and then, taking her with them, continue through the moonlight their vain and anguished search. Krishna still evades them and they return to the terrace where the night's dancing had begun. There they once again implore Krishna to have pity, declaring that there is none like him in charm, that he is endlessly fascinating and that in all of them he has aroused extremities of passionate love. But the night is empty, their cries go unanswered, and moaning for the Krishna they adore, they toss and writhe on the ground.

At last, Krishna relents. He stands among them and seeing him, their cares vanish 'as creepers revive when sprinkled with the water of life.' Some of the cowgirls hardly dare to be angry but others

[1] Plate 13.   [2] Plate 14.   [3] Plate 15.

upbraid him for so brusquely deserting them. To all, Krishna gives the same answer. He is not to be judged by ordinary standards. He is a constant fulfiller of desire. It was to test the strength of their love that he left them in the forest. They have survived this stringent test and convinced him of their love. The girls are in no mood to query his explanation and 'uniting with him' they overwhelm him with frantic caresses.

Krishna now uses his 'delusive power' in order to provide each girl with a semblance of himself. He asks them to dance and then projects a whole series of Krishnas. 'The cowgirls in pairs joined hands and Krishna was in their midst. Each thought he was at her side and did not recognize him near anyone else. They put their fingers in his fingers and whirled about with rapturous delight. Krishna in their midst was like a lovely cloud surrounded by lightning. Singing, dancing, embracing and loving, they passed the hours in extremities of bliss. They took off their clothes, their ornaments and jewels and offered them to Krishna. The gods in heaven gazed on the scene and all the goddesses longed to join. The singing mounted in the night air. The winds were stilled and the streams ceased to flow. The stars were entranced and the water of life poured down from the great moon. So the night went on—on and on—and only when six months were over did the dancers end their joy.'

As, at last, the dance concludes, Krishna takes the cowgirls to the Jumna, bathes with them in the water, rids himself of fatigue and then after once again gratifying their passions, bids them go home. When they reach their houses, no one is aware that they have not been there all the time.

(iii) *The Death of the Tyrant*

This scene with its crescendos of excitement, its delight in physical passion and ecstatic exploration of sexual desire is, in many ways, the climax of Krishna's pastoral career. It expresses the devotion felt for him by the cowgirls. It stresses his loving delight in their company. It suggests the blissful character of the ultimate union. No further revelation, in fact, is necessary for this is the crux of Krishna's life. None the less the ostensible reason for his birth remains—to rid the earth of the vicious tyrant Kansa—and to this the *Purana* now returns.

We have seen how in his anxious quest for the child who is to kill him, Kansa has dispatched his demon warriors on roving commissions, authorizing them to attack and kill all likely children. Many children have in this way been slaughtered but Kansa is still uncertain whether his prime purpose has been fulfilled. He has no certain knowledge that among the dead children is his dreaded enemy. He is still unaware that Krishna is destined to be his foe and he therefore continues the hunt, his demon emissaries pouncing like commandos on youthful stragglers and hounding them to their deaths. Among such youths Krishna is still an obvious target and although unaware that this is the true object of their quest, demons continue to harry him.

One night Krishna and Balarama are in the forest with the cowgirls when a yaksha demon, Sankhasura, a jewel flashing in his head, comes among them. He drives the cowgirls off but hearing their cries, Krishna follows after. Balarama stays with the girls while Krishna catches and beheads the demon.

On another occasion, Krishna and Balarama are returning at evening with the cows when a bull demon careers amongst them. He runs amok scattering the cattle in all directions. Krishna, however, is not at all daunted and after wrestling with the bull, catches its horns and breaks its neck.

To such blind attacks there is no immediate end. One day, however, a sage discloses to Kansa the true identity of his enemy. He tells him in what manner Balarama and Krishna were born, how Balarama was transferred from Devaki's womb to that of Rohini, and how Krishna was transported to Nanda's house in Gokula. Kansa is now confronted with the ghastly truth—how Vasudeva's willingness to surrender his first six sons has lulled his suspicions, how his confidence in Vasudeva has been entirely misplaced, and how completely he has been deceived. He sends for Vasudeva and is on the point of killing him when the sage interposes, advising Kansa to imprison Vasudeva for the present and meanwhile make an all-out attempt to kill or capture Balarama and Krishna. Kansa sees the force of his remarks, spares Vasudeva for the moment, throws him and Devaki into jail and dispatches a special demon, the horse Kesi, on a murderous errand.

As the horse speeds on its way, Kansa assembles his demon councillors, explains the situation to them and asks for their advice. If Krishna should not be killed in the forest, the only alternative, the demons suggest, is to decoy him to Mathura. Let a handsome theatre be built, a sacrifice to Siva held and a special festival of arms proclaimed. All the cowherds will naturally come to see it. Nanda, the rich herdsman, will bring presents, Krishna and Balarama will come with other cowherds. When they have arrived the wrestler

Chanura can throw them down and kill them. Kansa is delighted at the suggestion, adding only that a savage elephant should be stationed at the gate ready to tear Krishna and Balarama to pieces immediately they enter. He then dismisses his demon advisers and sends for Akrura, the chief of the Yadavas and a leading member of his court. Akrura, he judges, will be the best person to decoy Krishna to Mathura. He accordingly briefs him as to his intentions and instructs him to await orders. Akrura deems it politic to express compliance but secretly is overjoyed that he will thus obtain access to the Krishna he adores.

The first stage of Kansa's master plan is now brought into effect. The horse demon, Kesi, reaches Brindaban and begins to paw the ground and kick up its heels. The cowherds are frightened but Krishna dares it to attack. The horse tries to bite him but Krishna plunges his hand down its throat and expands it to a vast size until the demon bursts. Its remains litter the ground but Krishna is so unmoved that he merely summons the cowherd children to play a game. Squatting with them under a fig tree, he names one of them a general, another a minister, a third a councillor and himself pretending to be a raja plays with them at being king. A little later they join him in a game of blind man's buff.

This unexpected *dénouement* enrages Kansa but instead of desisting from the attempt and bringing into force the second part of his plan, he decides to make one further effort to murder his hated foe. He accordingly summons the wolf demon, Vyamasura, gives him detailed instructions and dispatches him to Brindaban. The demon hies to the forest, arriving while Krishna and the children are still at blind man's buff. He has dressed himself as a beggar and going humbly up to Krishna asks if he may join in. Krishna tells him to choose whatever game he likes and the demon says, 'What about the game of wolf and rams?' 'Very well,' Krishna answers, 'You be the wolf and the cowherd boys the rams.' They start to play and the demon rounds up all the children and keeps them in a cave. Then, assuming true wolf's form he pounces on Krishna. Krishna, however, is quite prepared and seizing the wolf by the throat, strangles it to death.

Akrura is now sent for and instructed to go to Brindaban and return with Krishna to Mathura. He sets out and as he journeys allows his thoughts to dwell on the approaching meeting. 'Now,' he muses 'has my life borne fruit; my night is followed by the dawn of day; since I shall see the countenance of Vishnu, whose eyes are like the expanded leaf of the lotus. I shall behold that lotus-eyed aspect of Vishnu, which, when seen only in imagination, takes away the sins of men. I shall today behold that glory of glories, the mouth of Vishnu, whence proceeded the Vedas, and all their dependent sciences. I shall see the sovereign of the world, by whom the world is sustained; who is worshipped as the best of males, as the male sacrifice in sacrificial rites. I shall see Vishnu, who is without beginning or end; by worshipping whom with a hundred sacrifices, Indra obtained the sovereignty over the gods. The soul of all, the knower of all, he who is all and is present in all, he who is permanent, undecaying, all-pervading will converse with me. He, the unborn, who has preserved the world in the various forms of a fish, tortoise, a boar, a horse, a lion will this day speak to me. Now the lord of the earth, who assumes shapes at will, has taken upon him the condition of humanity, to accomplish some object cherished in his heart. Glory to that being whose deceptive adoption of father, son, brother, friend, mother, and relative, the world is unable to penetrate. May he in whom cause and effect, and the world itself, is comprehended, be propitious to me, through his truth; for always do I put my trust in that unborn, eternal Vishnu; by meditation on whom man becomes the repository of all good things.'[1]

He goes on to think of how he will kneel before Krishna with folded hands and afterwards put on his head the dust of Krishna's feet—the same feet which 'have come to destroy crime, which fell on the snake Kaliya's head and which have danced with the cowgirls in the forest.' Krishna, he believes, will know at once that he is not Kansa's envoy and will receive him with kindness. And this is what actually ensues. Meeting Krishna outside Brindaban, he falls at his feet, Krishna lifts him up, embraces him and brings him into Nanda's house. Akrura tells Nanda and Krishna how Kansa has oppressed the people of Mathura, imprisoned Vasudeva and Devaki and has now sent him to invite them to attend the festival of arms. Krishna listens and at once agrees to go, while Nanda sends out a town-crier to announce by beat of drum that all the cowherds should get ready to leave the next day. When morning comes, Krishna leaves in a chariot, accompanied by the cowherds and their children.

The news of his sudden departure devastates the cowgirls. Since the circular dance in which their love was consummated, they have been meeting Krishna every evening and delighting in his company. And during the daytime their passionate longings have centred solely on him. That he should leave them so abruptly causes them

[1] Note 7.

complete dismay and they are only comforted when Krishna assures them that he will return after a few days.

On the way to Mathura Akrura bathes in the Jumna and is granted a vision of Krishna as Vishnu himself.

Reaching Mathura, Nanda and the cowherds pitch their tents outside the city walls[1] while Krishna with Balarama and the cowherd children go inside the city for a walk. As they wander through the streets, the news of their arrival precedes them and women, excited by Krishna's name, throng the rooftops, balconies and windows. 'Some ran off in the middle of their dinner: others while bathing and others while engaged in plaiting their hair. They forgot all dalliance with their husbands and went to look at Krishna.' As Krishna proceeds, he meets some of Kansa's washermen carrying with them bundles of clothes. He asks them to give him some and when they refuse, he attacks one of them and strikes off his head. The others drop their bundles and run for their lives. The cowherd children try to dress themselves up but not knowing how to wear the clothes, some of them put their arms into trousers and their legs into coats. Krishna laughs at their mistakes until a tailor, a servant of Kansa, repudiates his master, glorifies Krishna and sets the clothes right. A little later, a gardener takes them to his house and places garlands round their necks. As they are leaving, they meet a young woman, a hunchback, carrying a pot of scented ointment. Krishna cannot resist flirting with her and asks her for whom she is carrying the ointment. The girl, Kubja, sees the amorous look in his eyes and being greatly taken by his beauty answers 'Dear one, do you not know that I am a servant of Raja Kansa and though a hunchback am entrusted with making his perfumes?' 'Lovely one,' Krishna answers, 'Give us a little of this ointment, just enough to rub on our bodies.' 'Take some,' says Kubja, and giving it to Krishna and Balarama, she allows them to rub it on their bodies. When they have finished, Krishna takes her under the chin, lifts her head and at the same time, presses her feet down with his toes. In this way he straightens her back, thereby changing her into the loveliest of girls. Filled with love and gratitude, Kubja catches Krishna by the dress and begs him to come and visit her. Krishna promises to go later and smilingly dismisses her.

Krishna now reaches the gate where the bow of Siva 'as long as three palm trees' and very heavy, is being guarded by soldiers. He picks it up, bends it to the full and breaks it in pieces. When the guards attack him, he kills them and presently slaughters all the

[1] Plate 16.

reinforcements which Kansa sends. When the battle is over, he strolls calmly back to the cowherds' tents.[1]

Next day, Krishna and the cowherds enter Mathura to attend the sports. Krishna is obstructed by a giant elephant, attacks it and after a great fight kills it. He and Balarama then extract the tusks and parade with them in the arena. It is now the turn of Kansa's wrestlers. Their leader, Chanura, dares Krishna to give Kansa a little amusement by wrestling with him. Krishna takes him at his word and again after a fierce combat leaves the wrestler dead on the ground.[2] At the same time, Balarama attacks and kills a second wrestler, Mustaka. When other wrestlers strive to kill Krishna and Balarama, they also are dispatched. Seeing first one and then another plan go astray, Kansa orders his remaining demons to fetch Vasudeva, Devaki and Ugrasena, declaring that after he has killed them he will put the two young men to death. This declaration seals his fate. In a flash Krishna slays Kansa's demons and then, leaping on the dais where Kansa is sitting, he seizes him by the hair and hurls him to the ground. Kansa is killed and all Mathura rejoices. Kansa's eight demon brothers are then slain and only when Krishna has dragged Kansa's body to the river Jumna and is sure that not a single demon is left do he and Balarama desist from fighting.

[1] Plate 16.   [2] Plate 17.

IV

THE *BHAGAVATA PURANA:* THE PRINCE

(i) *The Return to Court*

The death of Kansa brings to a close the first phase of Krishna's career. His primary aim has now been accomplished. The tyrant whose excesses have for so long vexed the righteous is dead. Earth's prayer has been granted. Krishna has reached, in fact, a turning-point in his life and on what he now decides the rest of his career depends. If he holds that his earthly mission is ended, he must quit his mortal body, resume his sublime celestial state and once again become the Vishnu whose attributes have been praised by Akrura when journeying to Brindaban. If, on the other hand, he regards his mission as still unfulfilled, is he to return to Brindaban or should he remain instead at Mathura? At Brindaban, his foster parents, Nanda and Yasoda, his friends the cowherds and his loves the cowgirls long for his return. He has spent idyllic days in their company. He has saved them from the dangers inherent in forest life. He has kept a host of demon marauders at bay. At the same time, his magnetic charms have aroused the most intense devotion. If he returns, it will be to dwell with people who have doted on him as a child, adored him as a youth and who love him as a man. On the other hand, Mathura, it is clear, has also strong claims. Although reared and bred among the cowherds, Krishna is, in fact, a child of Mathura. Although smuggled from the prison immediately afterwards, it was in Mathura that he left his mother's womb. His true father is Vasudeva, a leader of the Yadava nobility and member of the Mathura ruling caste. His true mother, Devaki, is related to the Mathura royal family. If his youth and infancy have been passed among the cowherds, this was due to special reasons. His father's substitution of him at birth for Yasoda's baby daughter was dictated by the dire perils which would have confronted him had he remained with his mother. It was, at most, a desperate expedient for saving his life and although the tyrant's unremitting search for the child who was to kill him prolonged his stay in Brindaban, his transportation there was never intended as a permanent arrangement. A deception has been practised. Nanda and Yasoda regard and believe

Krishna to be their son. None the less there has been no formal adoption and it is Vasudeva and Devaki who are his parents.

It is this which decides the issue. As one who by birth and blood belongs to Mathura, Krishna can hardly desert it now that the main obstacle to his return—the tyrant Kansa—has been removed. His plain duty is to his parents and his castemen. Painful therefore as the severance must be, he decides to abandon the cowherds and see them no more. He is perhaps fortified in his decision by the knowledge that even in his relations with the cowgirls a climax has been reached. A return would merely repeat their nightly ecstasies, not achieve a fresh experience. Finally although Kansa himself has been killed, his demon allies are still at large. Mathura and Krishna's kinsmen, the Yadavas, are far from safe. He can hardly desert them until their interests have been permanently safeguarded and by then he will have become a feudal princeling, the very reverse of the young cowherd who night after night has thrilled the cowgirls with his flute.

Following the tyrant's death, then, a train of complicated adjustments are set in motion. The first step is to re-establish Krishna with his true parents who are still in jail where the tyrant has confined them. Krishna accordingly goes to visit them, frees them from their shackles and stands before them with folded hands. For an instant Vasudeva and Devaki know that Krishna is God and that in order to destroy demons he has come on earth. They are about to worship him when Krishna dispels this knowledge and they look on him and Balarama as their sons. Then Krishna addresses them. For all these long years Vasudeva and Devaki have known that Krishna and Balarama were their children and have suffered accordingly. It was not Krishna's fault that he and Balarama were placed in Nanda's charge. Yet although parted from their mother, they have never forgotten her. It pains them to think that they have done so little to make her happy, that they have never had her society and have wasted their time with strangers. And he reminds them that in the world only those who serve their fathers and mothers obtain power. Vasudeva and Devaki are greatly touched by Krishna's words. Their former woe vanishes and they embrace Krishna and Balarama fondly.

Having acknowledged Vasudeva and Devaki as his true parents, Krishna has now to adjust his social position. Since Nanda and the cowherds belong to a lower caste than that of Vasudeva and the other Yadavas, Krishna and Balarama, who have eaten and drunk with the cowherds and have been brought up with them, are not true members of the Yadava community. The family priest is accordingly consulted and it is decided that a ceremony for admitting them into caste must be performed. This is done and Krishna and Balarama are given the customary sacred threads. They are now no longer cowherds but true Yadavas. At the same time they are given a spiritual preceptor who instructs them in the sacred texts and manuals of learning. When they have finished the course, they express their gratitude by restoring to him his dead son who has been drowned in the sea.

One further obligation springs from their new position. We have seen how in the epic, the *Mahabharata*, Krishna stands in a special relation to the Pandavas, the faction which emerges victorious from the great feud. The mother of the Pandavas is called Kunti and it is Kunti who is the sister of Krishna's father, Vasudeva. Since he is now with his true father, rumours concerning Kunti reach Krishna and he learns that along with her sons, the five Pandavas, she is being harassed by the Kaurava king, the blind Dhritarashtra, egged on by his son, the evil Duryodhana. Being now a part of his father's family, Krishna can hardly be indifferent to the fate of so intimate a relative. Akrura, the leading Yadava diplomat, whom the tyrant had employed to bring Krishna to Mathura, is accordingly despatched on yet another mission. He is to visit the Kauravas and Pandavas, ascertain the facts, console Krishna's aunt, Kunti, and then return and report. Akrura reaches the Kauravas' capital and discovers that the rumours are only too correct. Relations between the two families are strained to breaking point. The blind king is at the mercy of his son, Duryodhana, and it is the latter who is ceaselessly harrying Kunti and her sons. A little later, as we have already seen, a final attempt on their lives will be made, they will be induced to sleep in a new house, the house will be fired and only by a fortunate chance will the Pandavas escape to the forest and dwell in safety. This, however, is in the future and for the moment Kunti and her sons are still at court. Akrura assures Kunti of Krishna's abiding concern and returns to Mathura. Krishna and Balarama are perturbed to hear his news, deliberate on whether to intervene, but decide for the moment to do nothing.

The second adjustment which Krishna has now to make is to reconcile the cowherds to his permanent departure from them and to wean them from their passionate adherence to his presence. This is much more difficult. We have seen how on the journey to Mathura, Krishna has been accompanied by Nanda and the cowherds and how during the closing struggle with the tyrant they also have been present. When the fight is finally over, they prepare to depart, taking it for granted that Krishna and Balarama will come with them. Krishna has therefore to disillusion Nanda. He breaks the news to him that it is not he and Yasoda who are actually his parents but Vasudeva and Devaki. He loads Nanda with jewels and costly dresses and thanks him again and again for all his loving care. He then explains that he has now to stay in Mathura for a time to meet his castemen, the Yadavas. Nanda is greatly saddened by the news. The cowherds strive to dissuade him but Krishna is adamant. He retains a few cowherds with him, but the rest return to Brindaban, Krishna promising that after a time he will visit them. On arrival Nanda strives in vain to console Yasoda and is forced to tell her that Krishna has now acknowledged Vasudeva as his true father, that he has probably left Brindaban for good and that his own early intuition that Krishna was God is correct. Yasoda, as she thinks of her lost 'son,' is overwhelmed with grief, but recovers when she realizes that actually he is God. As to the cowgirls, their grief is endless as they recall Krishna's heart-ensnaring charms.

Such a step is obviously only the first move in what must necessarily be a long and arduous operation. Finding it impossible to say outright that he will never see them again, Krishna has committed himself to paying the cowherds a visit. Yet he realizes that nothing can be gained by such a step since, if his future lies with the princely Yadavas, any mingling with the cowherds will merely disrupt this final role. Yet clearly he cannot just abandon his former associates without any regard at all for their proper feelings. Weaning is necessary, and it must above all be gradual. He decides, therefore, that since he himself cannot go, someone must be sent on his behalf. Accordingly, he instructs a friend, Udho, to go to Brindaban, meet the cowherds and make excuses for his absence. At the same time, he must urge the cowgirls to give up regarding Krishna as their lover but worship him as God. Udho is accordingly dressed in Krishna's clothes, thereby making him appear a real substitute and is despatched in Krishna's chariot.

When Udho arrives, he finds Nanda and Yasoda still lamenting Krishna's absence and the cowgirls still longing for him as their lover. He begs them to regard Krishna as God—as someone who is constantly near those who love him even if he cannot be seen. Krishna, he says, has forbidden them to hope for any further impassioned ecstasies and now requires them to offer him their devotion only. If they do penance and meditate, Krishna will never leave them. From the day they commenced thinking of him, none have been so much loved as they. 'As earth, wind, water, fire, rain dwell in the body, so Krishna dwells in you; but through the influence of his delusive power seems to be apart.' Udho's pleading shocks and embitters the cowgirls. 'How can he talk to us like that?' they ask. 'It is Krishna's body that we adore, not some invisible idea high up in the sky. How has Krishna suddenly become invisible and imperceptible, a being without qualities and form, when all along he has delighted us with his physical charms. As to penance and meditation, these concern widows. What woman does penance while her husband is alive? It is all the doing of Kubja, the girl of Mathura whose charms have captivated Krishna. Were it not for Kubja and other beauties of Mathura, Krishna would now be with us in Brindaban. Had we known he would not return, we would never have let him go.' In such words they repudiate Udho's message, upbraid Krishna for his fickle conduct and demonstrate with what intensity they still adore him.

Udho is reduced to silence and can only marvel at the cowgirls' bliss in abandoning everything to think only of Krishna. Finally they send Krishna the message—that if he really desires them to abandon loving him with their bodies and resort to penance, he himself must come and show them how to do it. Unless he comes, they will die of neglect.

A few days later, Udho returns to Mathura bringing with him milk and butter as presents to Krishna from Nanda and Yasoda and escorting Rohini, Vasudeva's other wife and Balarama's mother. He gives Krishna the cowgirls' message and reports how all Brindaban longs for his return. 'Great King,' he says, 'I cannot tell you how they love you. You are their life. Night and day they think of you. Their love for you is complete as perfect worship. I gave them your advice concerning penance, but I have learnt from them perfect adoration. They will only be content when they see and touch you again.' Krishna listens and is silent. It is clear that efforts at weaning the cowgirls from him have so far failed and something further must be attempted.

Yet his resolve to sever all connections with his former life remains and it is perhaps symbolic of his purpose that he now recalls the hunch-back girl, Kubja, takes Udho with him and in a single ecstatic visit becomes her lover. As he reaches her house, the girl greets him with delight, takes him inside and seats him on a couch of flowers. Udho stays outside and then while Krishna waits, the girl quickly bathes, scents herself, combs her hair and changes her dress. Then 'with gaiety and endearment' she approaches Krishna.

Krishna, however, takes her by the hand and places her near him. Their passions rise and the two achieve the utmost bliss. Krishna then leaves her, rejoins Udho and 'blushing and smiling' returns home.

The third step which Krishna must take is to deal with the political and military situation which has arisen from the slaying of the tyrant. We have seen how Kansa, although actually begotten by a demon was officially a son of Ugrasena, the king of Mathura, and as one of his many demon acts, had dethroned his father and seized the kingdom for himself. Ugrasena is still alive and the obvious course, therefore, is to reinstate him on the throne. Ugrasena, however, is unwilling to assume power and he and the other Yadavas implore Krishna to accept the title for himself. Krishna, however, has no desire to become king. He therefore overcomes Ugrasena's hesitations and in due course the latter is enthroned.

This settles the succession problem, but almost immediately a graver issue arises. During his reign of terror, Kansa had made war on Jarasandha, king of Magadha. He had defeated him but as part of the peace terms had taken two of his daughters as queens. These have now been widowed by his death and repairing to their father's court, they rail bitterly against Krishna and beg their father to avenge their husband's death. Jarasandha, although a former rival of Kansa, is also a demon and can therefore summon to his aid a number of demon allies. Great armies are accordingly mobilized. Mathura is surrounded and the Yadavas are in dire peril. Krishna and Balarama, however, are undismayed. They attack the foes single-handed and by dint of their supernatural powers, utterly rout them. Jarasandha is captured but released so that he may return to the attack and even more demons may then be slaughtered. He returns in all seventeen times, is vanquished on each occasion but returns once more. This time he is aided by another demon, Kalayavana, and seeing the constant strain of such attacks, Krishna decides to evacuate the Yadavas and settle them at a new base. He commissions the divine architect, Visvakarma, to build a new city in the sea. This is done in one night, the city is called Dwarka[1] and there the Yadavas with all their goods are transported. When this has been done, Krishna and Balarama trick the demons. They pretend to be utterly defeated, retreat from Mathura and in despair ascend a tall hill. The demon armies surround them and there appears to be no possible way of escape. Jarasandha orders wood to be brought from the surrounding towns and villages, piled up

[1] Dwarka is sited on the western seaboard, 300 miles north-west of Bombay.

round the hill, saturated with oil and then set fire to. A vast flame shoots up. The whole hill is ablaze but Krishna and Balarama slip out unseen, take the road to Mathura and finally reach Dwarka. When the hill is reduced to ashes, Jarasandha concludes that Krishna and Balarama have perished. He advances to Mathura, occupies the empty town, proclaims his authority and returns to Magadha.

(ii) *Marriages and Offspring*

The immediate position, then, is that Krishna has abandoned his life among the cowherds, has been accepted as a Yadava, has coped with the difficult and dangerous situation arising from the tyrant king's death and finally has saved the Yadavas from extinction by demons. This, however, has meant the abandonment of Mathura and the movement of the Yadavas to a new city, Dwarka. The same problem, therefore, which faced him earlier, confronts him once again. Having obtained immunity for the Yadavas and brought them to a new land, can Krishna now regard his mission as accomplished? Or must he linger on earth still longer? The answer can hardly be in doubt; for although the Yadavas appear to be installed in good surroundings, demon hordes still range the world. The tyrant Kansa was only the worst and most powerful member of the demon hosts. The war with Jarasandha has rid the world of many demons, but vast numbers remain and until their ranks have been appreciably reduced, Krishna's mission will be unfulfilled. Only one course of action, therefore, is possible. He must accept a permanent position in Yadava society, live as an honoured noble, a prince of the blood royal and as occasion warrants continue to intervene in the struggle between the good and the bad.

Such a decision is taken and Krishna installs himself at Dwarka. Before he can fulfil his duties as an adult member of the race, however, certain preliminaries are necessary and among them is the important issue of his marriage. Both he and Balarama require wives and the question is how are they to get them. Balarama's problem is easily settled by a marriage to Revati, a princess. Krishna's, on the other hand, is less straightforward and he is still undecided when news is brought that the Raja of Kundulpur has a daughter of matchless loveliness, her name Rukmini. Her eyes, it was said, were like a doe's, her complexion like a flower, her face dazzling as the moon. Rukmini in turn has overheard some beggars reciting Krishna's exploits, has fallen in love with his image and is at once delighted and disturbed. In this way each is fascinated by the other. Almost immediately, however, a crisis occurs. Rukmini's brother, Rukma, urges her father to marry her to a rival, Sisupala. Krishna's claims as Vishnu incarnate are advanced in vain and he is ridiculed as being just a cowherd. Against his better judgment her father acquiesces and arrangements for a wedding with Sisupala go forward. Rukmini now takes the daring step of sending a message to Krishna, declaring her love and asking him to save her. Krishna reads it with delight. He at once leaves for Kundulpur, finding it gay with flags and banners, golden spires and wreaths of flowers. Sisupala has arrived, but in addition, there is Krishna's old enemy, Jarasandha, encamped with an army of demons. Rukmini is in despair until she learns that Krishna also has arrived. A little later Balarama reaches the scene, bringing with him an army. Sisupala is dismayed at his arrival and both sides watch each other's movements. The wedding day now dawns and Rukmini, guarded by Sisupala's soldiers, goes outside the city to worship at a shrine to Devi.[1] As she nears the shrine, Krishna suddenly appears. Rukmini gazes with adoration at him. He springs among the soldiers, lifts her into his chariot and rushes her away.

This summary abduction is more than Sisupala can bear. Troops career after Krishna. Armies engage. A vast battle ensues. As they fight, Rukmini looks timorously on. At last, Balarama vanquishes the demon hosts, 'as a white elephant scatters lotuses.' Sisupala and Jarasandha flee, but Rukmini's evil brother, Rukma, returns to the fray, strives feverishly to kill Krishna, fails and is taken captive. His life is spared at Rukmini's behest, but he is led away, his hands tied behind his back and his moustaches shaven off. Balarama intercedes and effects his release and Rukma goes away to brood on his discomfiture and plot revenge. Krishna now returns to Dwarka in triumph, is given a rapturous welcome and a little later celebrates his marriage with full ritual. 'Priests recited the Vedas, Krishna circled round with Rukmini. Drums resounded. The delighted gods rained down flowers; demi-gods, saints, bards and celestial musicians were all spectators from the sky.'

Having married Rukmini, Krishna has now the full status of a grown prince. But he is nothing if not supernormal; and just as earlier in his career he has showered his affection on a host of cowgirls, he now acquires a whole succession of further wives. The first is Jambhavati, the second Satyabhama. Satyabhama's father is a certain Sattrajit who has obtained from the sun the boon of a jewel. The jewel flashes with light and Krishna advises him to surrender it

[1] Plate 18.

to King Ugrasena. The man refuses; whereupon his brother seizes it and goes away to the forest. Here a lion pounces upon him, devours the man and his horse and hides the jewel. The lion is then killed by a bear who centuries earlier had served with Vishnu's earlier incarnation, Rama, during his campaign against the demon king of Lanka.[1] The bear carries away the jewel and gives it to its mate. When Sattrajit hears that his brother is missing, he concludes that Krishna has caused his death and starts a whispering campaign, accusing Krishna of making away with the jewel. Krishna hears of the slander and at once decides to search for the missing man, recover the jewel and thus silence his accuser for ever. As he goes through the forest, Krishna finds a cave where the dead lion is lying. He enters it, grapples with the bear but is quickly recognized by the bear as Krishna himself. The bear bows before him and begs him to accept his daughter Jambhavati in marriage. He includes the jewel as part of the dowry. Krishna marries the girl and returns. Back at the court he upbraids Sattrajit for falsely accusing him. 'I did not take the jewel,' he says. 'The bear took it. Now he has given the jewel to me and also his daughter. Take back your jewel and be silent.' Sattrajit is overwhelmed with shame and by way of amends gives Krishna his own daughter, Satyabhama. Krishna marries her and Sattrajit begs him to take the jewel also. Krishna refuses and the jewel remains with its owner. A little later, Sattrajit is murdered and the jewel once again stolen. The murderer thief is tracked down by Krishna and killed, but only after many delays is the jewel at last recovered from Akrura—the leading Yadava who earlier in the story has acted first as Raja Kansa's envoy to Krishna and later as Krishna's envoy to Kunti. Krishna orders him to return it to its owner, Sattrajit's grandson. Akrura places it at Krishna's feet and Krishna gives it to Satyabhama. The upshot, then, is that the slander is ended, the jewel is regained and in the process Krishna acquires two further wives.

These extra marriages, however, by no means end the tally of his consorts, for during a visit to his relatives, the Pandavas, now returned from exile and for the moment safely reinstalled in their kingdom, he sees a lovely girl, Kalindi, wandering in the forest. She is the daughter of the sun and has been sent to dwell by a river until her appointed bridegroom, Krishna, arrives to claim her. Krishna is delighted with her youth, places her in his chariot and on his return to Dwarka, celebrates their wedding. A little later other girls are married to him, in many cases only after a fierce

[1] Lanka—modern Ceylon.

struggle with demons. In this way, he obtains eight queens, at the same time advancing his prime purpose of ridding the world of demons.

At this point, the *Purana* embarks on an episode which, at first sight, appears to have very little to do with its main subject. In fact, however, its relevance is great for, as a consequence, Krishna the prince acquires as many female companions as he had enjoyed as a youth. The episode begins with Earth again appearing in heaven. Having successfully engineered Krishna's birth, she does special penance and again beseeches the supreme Trinity to grant her a boon. This boon is a son who will never be equalled and who will never die. Brahma, Vishnu and Siva agree to give her a son, Naraka, but on the following conditions: he will conquer all the kings of the earth, rout the gods in the sky, carry off the earrings of Aditi (the mother of the gods), wear them himself, take the canopy of Indra and place it over his own head and finally, collect together but not marry sixteen thousand one hundred virgin daughters of different kings. Krishna will then attack him and at Earth's own behest, will kill Naraka and take to Dwarka all the imprisoned girls. Earth says, 'Why should I ever tell anyone to kill my own son?' and is silent. None the less the boon is granted, the conditions are in due course fulfilled and after a furious encounter with Naraka at his city of Pragjyotisha,[1] Krishna is once again victorious. During the battle, Muru or Mura, the arch demon, aided by seven sons, strenuously defends the city. Krishna kills him by cutting off his five heads but has then to resist whole armies of demons assembled by the sons. When these also have been destroyed, Krishna meets Naraka and after a vicious contest finally kills him, recovering in consequence the earrings of Aditi and the canopy of Indra. Naraka's palace is then opened and reveals the bevy of imprisoned girls. As they gaze on Krishna, their reactions are reminiscent of the cowgirls'. They implore Krishna to take them away and allow them to lavish on him their impassioned love. Krishna agrees, chariots are sent for and the vast concourse of passion-stricken girls is transported to Dwarka. Here Krishna marries them, showering affection on each of the sixteen thousand and one hundred 'and displaying unceasing love for his eight queens.'

Such an incident revives an aspect of Krishna's early character which up to the present has been somewhat obscured by other events. Besides slaying demons he has all along been sensitive to feminine needs, arousing in women passionate adoration and at the

[1] Note 12.

same time fulfilling the most intense of their physical desires. It is these qualities which characterize his later career.

Having on one occasion given Rukmini, his first consort, a flower of the heavenly wishing tree,[1] Krishna finds that he has aroused the jealousy of his third consort, Satyabhama. To please her, he accordingly undertakes to get for her not merely a flower or branch but the tree itself. He therefore goes to Vaikuntha, the paradise of Vishnu, and takes the opportunity to return the earrings of Aditi and place the canopy over the lord of the gods. He then sends a message to Indra asking for the tree. Indra as the tree's custodian recalls his former discomfiture in Brindaban when Krishna had abolished his worship and venerated the hill Govardhana in his place. Despite his subsequent surrender to Krishna, and abject worship of him, Indra is still incensed and bluntly refuses. Krishna then goes to the tree, wounds its guardians and bears the tree away. Indra is tempted to do battle but realizing Krishna's superior power calls off his hosts. Back in Dwarka, Krishna instals the tree in Satyabhama's palace but returns it to Indra a year later.

On another occasion, Krishna and Rukmini are making love on a golden bed in a palace bedecked with gems. The sheets are white as foam and are decorated with flowers. Pictures have been painted on the walls and every aid to pleasure has been provided. Rukmini is lovelier than ever, while Krishna, 'the root of joy,' dazzles her with a face lovely as the moon, a skin the colour of clouds, a peacock crown, a long garland of flowers and a scarf of yellow silk. As he lies, he is 'the sea of beauty, the light of the three worlds.' After making love, Krishna suddenly asks Rukmini why she preferred him to Sisupala. He points out that he is not a king and is therefore quite unworthy of her, that since he has rescued her from Sisupala, her wish has been accomplished and it is best that she should now leave him and marry a prince of the royal blood who will be worthy of her name. Rukmini is stunned at the suggestion. She collapses on the floor, her hair obscuring her lovely face. Krishna raises her up, sits her on his knees, and strokes her cheeks. When at length Rukmini revives, Krishna hastens to explain that he was only jesting and that in view of her deep love he will never abandon her. Rukmini assures him that nowhere in the world is there Krishna's equal. The beggars who recited his praises and from whom she first heard his name, were in fact Brahma and Siva. All the gods revere him. To adore him is the only joy. Those who love Krishna alone are happy. If

[1] A sight of the heavenly wishing-tree, the *kalpa* or *pariyata*, which grew in Indra's heaven, was believed to make the old young.

blinded by pride a man forgets him, Krishna abases him. It was because Rukmini besought his compassion that Krishna has loved her. Hearing her simple sincerity, Krishna is greatly moved and says, 'Love of my heart, you know me through and through. You have given yourself to me, adored me and known my love. I shall love you always.' Rukmini hears him with deep contentment and the two make love.

Such a declaration however is not intended to imply a cold neglect of his other wives for it is part of Krishna's role that he should please and satisfy all. Accordingly, when Narada, the sage, makes one of his recurring appearances—this time in order to investigate how Krishna contrives to keep happy so vast a concourse of women—he finds Krishna everywhere. With Rukmini he reclines at ease, with Jambhavati he plays dice, at Satyabhama's house, he is having his body rubbed with oil, at Kalindi's, he is asleep. In this way, wherever Narada goes, he finds Krishna with one or other of his queens. In fact, the same 'delusive' powers which he had earlier employed when dancing with the cowgirls—making each believe he was dancing with her and her alone—are now being used to satisfy his wives.

In this way Krishna continues to live. Sometimes his wives caress his body, ply him with delicacies or swathe him in perfumed garments. Sometimes to ease their passion they make little figures of him or let themselves be dressed by him. One night they go with him to a tank and there make love in the water. Everything in the scene reminds them of their love and they address first a *chakai* bird. 'O *chakai* bird, when you are parted from your mate, you spend the whole night sadly calling and never sleeping. Speak to us of your beloved. We are Krishna's slave-girls.' They speak to the sea. 'O sea, you lie awake night and day, heaving sighs. Do you grieve for a loved one who is far away?' Then they see the moon. 'O moon, why do you grow thin? Are you also filled with longing? Are you fascinated by Krishna?' In this way they address birds, hills and rivers, seeking from each some consolation for their frenzied love.

In due course, each of the sixteen thousand one hundred and eight bears Krishna ten sons and one daughter and each is beautiful as himself.

(iii) *Last Phases*

This gradual expansion of his marital state takes Krishna even farther from the adoring loves of his youth, the cowgirls of Brindaban. Indeed for months on end it is as if he has dismissed them from his mind. One day he and Balarama are sitting together when Balarama reminds him of their promise that after staying for a time in Mathura they will assuredly visit them. Krishna, it is clear, cannot go himself, but Balarama is less impeded and with Krishna's approval, he takes a ploughshare and pestle, mounts a chariot and speeds on his way.

As he nears Brindaban, the familiar scenes greet him. The cowherds and cowgirls come into view, but instead of joy there is general despair. The cows low and pant, rejecting the grass. The cowherds are still discussing Krishna's deeds and the cowgirls cannot expel him from their minds. As Balarama enters their house, Nanda and Yasoda weep with joy. Balarama is plied with questions about Krishna's welfare and when he answers that all is well, Yasoda describes the darkness that has descended on them since the joy of their hearts left. Balarama now meets the cowgirls. Their hair is disordered, they are no longer neat and smart. Their minds are not in their work and despite Krishna's absence, they are filled with passionate longings and frenzied desires. Some of them marvel at Krishna's love and count it good even to have known him. Others bitterly upbraid Krishna for deserting them. Balarama explains that his visit is to show them that Krishna has not entirely forgotten them and as proof he offers to re-enact the circular dance and himself engage with them as lover.

In this way the circular dance is once again performed. The full moon pours down, the cowgirls deck themselves and songs rise in the air. Flutes and drums play and in the midst of the throng Balarama sings and dances, clasping the cowgirls to him, making love and rousing them to ecstasy. Night after night the dance is performed, while each day Balarama comforts Nanda and Yasoda with news of Krishna. One night as his visit is ending, he feels exhausted and commands the river Jumna to change its course and bathe him with its water. The Jumna fails to comply, so Balarama draws the river towards him with his plough and bathes in its stream. From that time on, the Jumna's course is changed. His exhaustion now leaves him and he gratifies the cowgirls with fresh passion. With this incident his visit ends. He bids farewell to Nanda, Yasoda and the cowgirls and leaving the forest returns to Dwarka.

Krishna's relations with the cowgirls are now completely ended, but on one last occasion he happens to meet them. News has come that the sun will soon be eclipsed and accordingly, Krishna and Balarama take the Yadavas on pilgrimage. They choose a certain holy place, Kurukshetra, and assembling all their queens and wives, make the slow journey to it. When they arrive, a festival is in progress. They bathe and make offerings. While they are still encamped, other kings come in, including the Pandavas and Kauravas. With them are their wives and families and Kunti, the mother of the Pandavas, is thus enabled to meet once more her brother, Vasudeva, the father of Krishna. A little later, Nanda and Yasoda along with the cowherds and cowgirls also arrive. They have come on the same pilgrimage and finding Krishna there, at once throng to see him. Vasudeva greets his old friend, Nanda, and recalls the now long-distant days when Krishna had lived with him in his house. Krishna and Balarama greet Nanda and Yasoda with loving respect, while the cowgirls are excited beyond description. Krishna however refuses to regard them and faced with their ardent looks and impassioned adoration, addresses to them the following sermon. 'Whoever believes in me shall be fearlessly carried across the sea of life. You gave me your bodies, minds and wealth. You loved me with a love that knew no limit. No one has been so fortunate as you—neither Brahma nor Indra, neither any other god nor any man. For all along I have been living in you, loving you with a love that has never faltered. I live in everyone. What I say to you cannot easily be understood, but as light, water, fire, earth and air abide in the body, so does my glory.' To the cowgirls such words strike chill. But there is nothing they can say and when the festival is over, Krishna and the Yadavas return to Dwarka, while Nanda with the cowherds and cowgirls go back to Brindaban. This is the last time Krishna sees them.

This dismissal reveals how final is Krishna's severance from his former life, yet provided the cowherds are not involved, he is quick to honour earlier relationships. One day in Dwarka his mother, Devaki, tells him that she has a private grief—grief at the loss of the six elder brothers of Krishna slain by the tyrant Kansa. Krishna tells her not to mourn, descends to the third of the three worlds, interviews its ruler, Raja Bali, and effects the release of the six brothers. Returning with them, he gives them to his mother and her joy is great.

On another occasion he is visited by Sudama, a Brahman who had lived with him, when, after slaying the tyrant, he and Balarama had gone for instruction to their spiritual preceptor. Since then Sudama has grown thin and poor. The thatch on his hut has tumbled down. He has nothing to eat. His wife is alarmed at their abject state and advises him to seek out Krishna, his chief friend. 'If you go to him,' she says, 'our poverty will end because it is he who grants wealth and virtue, fulfils desires and bestows final happiness.' Sudama replies that even Krishna does not give anyone anything without that person giving him something first. As he has not given, how can he hope to receive? His wife then ties up a little rice in an old white cloth and gives it to Sudama as a present to Krishna. Sudama sets out. On reaching Dwarka, he is admitted to Krishna's presence, is immediately recognized and is treated with the utmost kindness and respect. Krishna himself washes his feet and reveres him as a Brahman.[1] 'Brother,' he says, 'from the time you quitted our preceptor's house, I have heard nothing of you. Your coming has purified my house and made me happy.' Krishna then notices the rice and laughingly asks Sudama what present his wife has sent him and why it is hidden under his arm. Sudama is greatly abashed but allows Krishna to take the bundle. On taking it, Krishna eats the rice. He then conducts Sudama within, feasts him on delicacies and puts him to bed. During the night he sends Visvakarma, the divine architect, to Sudama's home, with instructions to turn it into a palace. The next morning Sudama takes leave of Krishna, congratulating himself on not having asked Krishna for anything. As he nears home, he is dismayed to find no trace of his hut, but instead a golden palace. He approaches the gate-keeper and is told it belongs to Sudama, the friend of Krishna. His wife comes out and he finds her dressed in fine clothes and jewels and attended by maid-servants. She takes him in and at first he is abashed at so much wealth. Krishna, he reflects, can only have given it to him because he doubted his affection. He did not ask Krishna for wealth and cannot fathom why he has been given it. His wife assures him that Krishna knows the thoughts of everyone. Sudama did not ask for wealth, but she herself desired it and that is why Krishna has given it to them. Sudama is convinced and says no more.

All these incidents provide a clue to Krishna's nature. They illustrate his attitudes, confirm him in his role as protector and preserver and show him in a new light—that of a guardian and upholder of morality. He is still a fervent lover, but his love is sanctioned and formalized by legal marriage. Moreover, a new respect characterizes his dealings with Brahmans and his approach to festivals. Instead of the young revolutionary, we now meet a sage conservative. These changes colour his final career.

As life at Dwarka runs its course, Krishna's activities centre more and more on wars with demons and his relations with the Pandavas. Despite his prowess and renown, demons trouble the

[1] Plate 19.

Yadavas from time to time, but all are killed either by Krishna wielding a magic quoit or by Balarama plying his plough or pestle. On one occasion, a monkey demon runs amok, harassing the people and ravaging the country. He surprises Balarama bathing in a tank with his wives, despoils their clothes and defiles their pitchers. A great combat then ensues, the monkey hurling trees and hills while Balarama counters with his plough and pestle. But the outcome is hardly in doubt and at last the monkey is killed.

On another occasion, Krishna is compelled to intervene in force. Following his marriage with his first queen, Rukmini, a son, Pradyumna has been born. He is no less a person than Kama, the god of love, whom Siva has burnt for disturbing his meditations. When grown up, Pradyumna is married to a cousin, the daughter of his uncle, Rukma. Rukma has never forgiven Krishna for abducting and marrying his sister, Rukmini, and despite their intimate alliance is sworn to kill him. His plot is discovered and in a final contest, Balarama kills him. Meanwhile, Pradyumna has had a son, Aniruddha, who grows up into a charming youth, while at the same time Vanasura, a demon with a thousand arms, has a lovely daughter, Usa. When Usa is twelve years old, she longs for a husband and in a dream sees and embraces Aniruddha. She does not know who he is, but describes him to a confidante. The latter draws pictures of all the leading royalty, and among the Yadavas, Usa recognizes her love, Aniruddha. The confidante agrees to bring him to her and going through the air to Dwarka, finds him sleeping, dreaming of Usa. She transports him to Usa's palace and on waking, Aniruddha finds himself alone with his love. Usa conceals him, but the news reaches her father and he surrounds the palace with his demon army. Aniruddha routs the army but is caught by Vanasura, who then imprisons the two young lovers. News now reaches Krishna who rushes an army to the scene. A battle ensues during which Vanasura loses all his arms save four. He then worships Krishna, and Aniruddha and Usa are married.

Meanwhile Krishna is carefully maintaining relations with the Pandavas. We have seen how immediately after the slaying of the tyrant he sends an envoy to inquire after his aunt Kunti, the sister of his father, and mother of the five Pandavas. We have also noticed how during a visit to the Pandava court, he has acquired a new queen, Kalindi. He now embarks on several courses of action, each of which is designed to cement their relations. During a visit to his court, Arjuna, the brother whose lucky shot won Draupadi for the Pandavas, falls in love with Subhadra, Krishna's sister. Krishna is delighted to have him as a brother-in-law and as already narrated in the epic, he advises Arjuna to marry her by capture. A little later Krishna learns that Yudhisthira will shortly proclaim himself a 'ruler of the world' and decides to visit the Pandava court to assist at the sacrifice. He takes a vast army with him and advances on the court with massive splendour. As he arrives, he learns that Jarasandha whose feud is unabated has now imprisoned twenty thousand rajas, all of whom cry to be released. Krishna decides that Jarasandha's demon activities must be ended once for all and taking two of the Pandavas with him, Bhima and Arjuna, he sets out to destroy him. Jarasandha elects to engage Bhima in single-handed combat and for twenty-seven days the fight proceeds, each wielding a club and neither securing the advantage. Krishna now learns that Jarasandha can only be killed if he is split in two. He directs Bhima, therefore, to throw him down, place a foot on one of his thighs and catching the other leg with his hand, tear him asunder. Bhima does so and in this way Jarasandha is destroyed. The captive rajas are now released and after returning home they foregather at the Pandavas' court to assist at the sacrifice.

As arrangements proceed an incident occurs which illustrates yet again the complex situation arising from Krishna's dual character. Krishna is God, yet he is also man. Being a man, it is normally as a man that he is regarded. Yet from time to time particular individuals sense his Godhead and then he is no longer man but God himself. Even those, however, who view him as God do so only for brief periods of time and hence the situation is constantly arising in which Krishna is one moment honoured as God and then a moment later is treated as a man. And it is this situation which now recurs.

As we have already seen in the epic, part of the custom at imperial sacrifices was to offer presents to distinguished guests, and according to the epic the person chosen to receive the first present was Krishna himself. The *Purana* changes this by substituting gods for guests. Yudhisthira is uncertain who should be worshipped first. 'Who is the great lord of the gods,' he asks, 'to whom we should bow our heads?' To this a Pandava gives a clear answer. Krishna, he says, is god of gods. 'No one understands his nature. He is lord of Brahma, Siva and Indra. It is he who creates, preserves and destroys. His work is endless. He is the unseen and imperishable. He descends upon the earth continually for the sake of his worshippers and assuming mortal form appears and acts like a mortal. He sits in our houses and calls us 'brothers.' We are deluded by his power and consider him a brother. Yet never have we seen one as great as him.'

He speaks in fact as one who, knowing Krishna, has seen, for the moment, the god beyond the man. His vision is shared by the others present. Krishna is therefore placed on a throne and before the vast concourse of rajas, Yudhisthira worships him.

Among the guests, however, is one raja to whom the vision is denied. He is Sisupala, Krishna's rival for the hand of Rukmini, and since Rukmini's abduction, his deadly enemy. Krishna's elevation as a god is more than he can stomach and he utters an angry protest. Krishna, he says, is not god at all. He is a mere cowherd's son of low caste who has debased himself by eating the leavings of the cowherds' children and has even been the lover of the cowgirls. As a child he was an arrant pilferer, stealing milk and butter from every house, while as a youth he has trifled with other men's wives. He has also slighted Indra. Krishna quietly listens to this outburst. Then, deeming Sisupala's enmity to have reached its furthest limit, he allows his patience to be exhausted. He reaches for his quoit and hurling it through the air, slays Sisupala on the spot. The ceremonies are then completed and Krishna leaves for Dwarka. As he nears the city, he discovers the Yadavas hard pressed by an army of demons. He and Balarama intervene. The demons are either killed or put to flight and the Yadavas are rescued. When a little later Sisupala's two brothers bring an army against him, they too are vanquished.

Twelve years now intervene. Yudhisthira in the moment of triumph has gambled away his kingdom. The Pandavas have once again been driven into exile and the old feud has broken out afresh. As the exile ends, both sides prepare for war and Krishna also leaves for the battle. Balarama is loath to intervene so goes away on pilgrimage. After various adventures, however, he also arrives on the scene. As he comes, a series of single-handed combats is in progress with Krishna and other Rajas looking on. Duryodhana, the son of blind Dhritarashtra, the king of the Kauravas is fighting Bhima, the powerful Pandava and just as Balarama arrives he is dealt a foul blow and wounded in the thigh. Balarama is shocked to see so many uncles and cousins involved in strife and begs them to desist. Duryodhana replies that it is Krishna who has willed the war and that they are as puppets in his hands. It is Krishna who is actively aiding the Pandavas and the war is only being carried on because of his advice. It is Krishna also who has sponsored foul play. Balarama is pained at such accusations and strongly criticizes Krishna. Krishna, however, is ready with an answer. The Kauravas, he says, cheated the Pandavas of their kingdom by the game of dice.

Duryodhana had told Draupadi to sit on his thigh and so he deserved to have it broken. So unjust and tyrannical are the Kauravas that any methods used against them are fair. Balarama keeps silent and a little later returns to Dwarka.

This incident concludes the *Purana's* references to the war. Nothing is said of Krishna's sermon—the *Bhagavad Gita*. No mention is made of Krishna's role as charioteer to Arjuna. Nothing further is said of its deadly outcome. Krishna's career as a warrior, in fact, is ended and with this episode the *Purana* enters its final phase.

As Krishna lives at Dwarka, surrounded by his wives and huge progeny, he wearies of his earthly career. By now his mission has been accomplished. Hordes of demons have been slain, cruel monarchs killed and much of Earth's burden lifted. There is no longer any pressing need for him to stay and he decides to quit his body and 're-enter with all his emanations the sphere of Vishnu.' To do this, however, the whole of the Yadava race must first be ended.[1] One day some Yadava boys make fun of certain Brahmans. They dress up one of their company as a pregnant girl, take him to the Brahmans and innocently inquire what kind of child the woman will bring forth. The Brahmans immediately penetrate the disguise and angered at the youth's impertinence, they reply, 'A club that will crush the whole Yadava race.' The boys run to King Ugrasena, relate what has happened and are even more alarmed when an iron club is brought forth from the boy's belly. Ugrasena has the club ground to dust and thrown into the sea, where its particles become rushes. One part of the club, however, is like a lance and does not break. When thrown into the sea, it is swallowed by a fish. A hunter catches it and taking the iron spike from its stomach lays it aside for future use. It is an arrow made from this particular spike which a little later will bring about Krishna's death. Similarly it is the iron rushes which will cause the death of the Yadavas. Already, therefore, a chain of sinister happenings has been started and from now onwards the action moves relentlessly to its grim and tragic close.

As the final scene unfolds, the gods, headed by Brahma and Siva, approach Krishna begging him to return. Krishna tells them that everything is now in train and within seven nights he will complete the destruction of the Yadavas and return to his everlasting home.

Signs portending the destruction of Dwarka now appear. 'A dreadful figure, death personified, haunts every house, coming and going no one knows how and being invulnerable to weapons by which he is assailed. Strong hurricanes blow; large rats multiply and

[1] Note 13.

infest the roads and houses and attack persons in their sleep; starlings scream in their cages, storks imitate the hooting of owls and goats the howling of jackals; cows bring forth foals and camels mules; food in the moment of being eaten is filled with worms; fire burns with discoloured flames and at sunset and sunrise the air is traversed by headless and hideous spirits.'[1] Krishna draws the Yadavas' attention to these omens and advises them to leave Dwarka and move to Prabhasa, a site farther inland.

Udho, who earlier in the story has acted as Krishna's envoy to the cowgirls quickly realizes that the end is near and approaches Krishna for advice. 'Tell me, O Lord, what it is proper I should do. For it is clear that shortly you will destroy the Yadavas.' Krishna then tells him to go to a shrine high up in the mountains and by meditating on Krishna obtain release. He adds minute instructions on the technique of penance and ends with some definitions of the yoga of devotion. He concludes by telling Udho that when all the Yadavas have perished, he himself will go to heaven and Dwarka will be swallowed by the ocean. Udho bows low and leaves for the mountains.

Krishna now assembles the leading Yadavas and leaving behind only the elders, the women and children, escorts them to Prabhasa, a town inland, assuring them that by proper worship they may yet avert their fate. At Prabhasa the Yadavas bathe and purify themselves, anoint the gods' statues and make offerings. They appease the Brahmans with costly gifts—'thereby countering evil omens, gaining the road to happiness and ensuring rebirth at a higher level.'

Their worship however, is of no avail for almost immediately they fall to drinking. 'As they drank, the destructive flame of dissension was kindled amongst them by mutual collision, and fed with the fuel of abuse. Infuriated by the divine influence, they fell upon one another with missile weapons and when these were expended, they had recourse to the rushes growing high. The rushes in their hands became like thunderbolts and they struck one another with them fatal blows. Krishna interposed to prevent them but they thought that he was taking part with each severally, and continued the conflict. Krishna then, enraged, took up a handful of rushes to destroy them, and the rushes became a club of iron and with this he slew many of the murderous Yadavas; whilst others, fighting fiercely, put an end to one another. In a short time, there was not a single Yadava left alive, except the mighty Krishna and Daruka, his charioteer.'[2]

[1] Note 14.   [2] Note 7.

With the slaughter thus completed, Krishna feels free to leave the earth. Such Yadavas who have been left behind in Dwarka have been spared, but the greater part of the race is dead. He therefore makes ready for his own departure. Balarama, who has helped Krishna in the brawl, goes to the sea-shore, performs yoga and, leaving his body, joins the Supreme Spirit. Sesha, the white serpent of eternity, issues from his mouth and hymned by snakes and other serpents proceeds to the ocean. 'Bringing an offering of respect, Ocean came to meet him; and then the majestic being, adored by attendant snakes entered into the waters of the deep.'[1]

Krishna then seats himself by a fig tree, lays his left leg across his right thigh, turns the sole of his foot outwards and assumes one of the postures in which abstraction is practised. As he meditates he appears lovelier than ever. His eyes flash. The four arms of Vishnu spring from his body. He wears his crown, his sacred thread and garland of flowers. As he sits, glorious and beautiful, the same hunter, who earlier had salvaged the iron spike from the fish, chances to pass by. His arrow is tipped with a piece of the iron and mistaking Krishna's foot for part of a deer, he shoots his arrow and hits it. Approaching the mark, he sees Krishna's four arms and is horrified to discover whom he has wounded. As he begs forgiveness, Krishna grants him liberation and dispatches him to heaven.

Daruka, Krishna's charioteer, now comes in search of his master. Finding him wounded, he is overwhelmed with grief. Krishna tells him to go to Dwarka and inform the surviving Yadavas what has happened. On receiving the news they must leave Dwarka immediately, for the sea will shortly engulf it. They must also place themselves under Arjuna's protection and go to Indraprastha. 'Then the illustrious Krishna having united himself with his own pure, spiritual, inexhaustible and universal spirit abandoned his mortal body.'[2]

Daruka goes mournfully to Dwarka where he breaks the news. Vasudeva with his two wives, Devaki and Rohini, die of grief. Arjuna recovers the bodies of Krishna and Balarama and places them on a funeral pyre. Rukmini along with Krishna's seven other queens throw themselves on the flames. Balarama's wives, as well as King Ugrasena, also die. Arjuna then appoints Krishna's great grandson, Parikshit, to rule over the survivors and, after assembling the remaining women and children, removes them from Dwarka and travels slowly away. As they leave, the ocean comes up, swallowing the city and engulfing everything except the temple.

[1] Plate 1 and Note 7.   [2] Plate 2 and Note 7.

(iv) *The* Purana *Re-considered*

Such an account gives us what the *Mahabharata* epic did not give—a detailed description of Krishna's career. It confirms the epic's view of Krishna as a hero and fills in many gaps concerning his life at Dwarka, his relations with the Pandavas, his life as a feudal prince and finally, his death. It makes clear that throughout the story Krishna is an incarnation of Vishnu and that his main reason for being born is to aid the good and kill demons. At the same time, it shows him in two important new lights—firstly, as one whose youth was spent among cowherds, in circumstances altogether different from those of a prince and secondly, as a delightful lover of women, who explores to the full the joys of sexual love. The second role characterizes him both as cowherd and prince but with important differences of attitude and behaviour. As a prince, Krishna is wedded first to Rukmini and then to seven other wives, observing on each occasion the requisite formalities. Even the sixteen thousand one hundred girls whom he rescues from imprisonment receive this formal status. With all of them Krishna enjoys a variety of sexual pleasures and their love is moral, respectable and approved. Krishna the prince, in fact, is Krishna the husband. Krishna the cowherd, on the other hand, is essentially a lover. The cowgirls whose impassioned love he inspires are all married and in consorting with them he is breaking one of the most solemn requirements of the moral code. The first relationship has the secure basis of conjugal duty, the second the daring adventurousness of romantic passion.

The same abrupt contrast appears between his character as a cowherd and his character as a prince. As a youth he mixes freely with the cowherds, behaving with an easy naturalness of manner and obtaining from them an intense devotion. This devotion is excited by everything he does and whether as a baby crying for the breast, a little boy pilfering butter or a young man teasing the married girls, he exerts a magnetic charm. At no time does he neglect his prime duty of killing demons but this is subordinated to his innocent delight in living. He is shown as impatient with old and stereotyped forms of worship, as scorning ordinary morality and treating love as paramount. Although he acts continually with princely dignity and is always aware of his true character as Vishnu, his impact on others is based more on the understanding of their needs than on their recognition of him as God. When, at times, Krishna the cowherd is adored as God, he has already been loved as a boy and a young man. In the later story, this early charm is missing. Krishna is frequently recognized to be God and is continually revered and respected as a man. His conduct is invariably resolute but there is a kind of statesmanlike formality about his actions. He is respectful towards ritual, formal observances and Brahmans while in comparison with his encounters with the cowgirls his relations with women have an air of slightly stagnant luxury. His wives and consorts lavish on him their devotion but the very fact that they are married removes the romantic element from their relationship.

Such vital differences are only partially resolved in the *Bhagavata Purana*. Representing as they do two different conceptions of Krishna's character, it is inevitable that the resulting account should be slightly biased in one direction or the other. The *Bhagavata Purana* records both phases in careful detail blending them into a single organic whole. But there can be little doubt that its Brahman authors were in the main more favourably inclined towards the hero prince than towards the cowherd lover. There is a tendency for the older Krishna to disparage the younger. Krishna the prince's subsequent meetings with the cowgirls are shown as very different from his rapturous encounters with them in the forest and the fact that his later career involves so sharp a separation from them indicates that the whole episode was somewhat frowned upon. This is especially evident from the manner in which Krishna addresses the cowgirls when they meet him during the eclipse of the sun. By this time he has become an ardent husband constantly satisfying his many wives. He is very far from having abjured the delights of the flesh. Yet for all his former loves who long for him so passionately he has only one message. They must meditate upon him in their minds. No dismissal could be colder, no treatment more calculatingly callous. And even the accounts of Krishna's love-making reflects this bias. The physical charms of the cowgirls are minimized and it is only the beauty of Rukmini which is stressed. It is clear, in fact, that however much the one tradition involved a break with morals, the second tradition shrank from countenancing adultery and it was this latter tradition which commanded the authors' approval. Finally, on one important issue, the *Purana* as a whole is in no doubt. Krishna's true consort is Rukmini. That Krishna's nature should be complemented by a cowgirl is not so much as even considered. The cowgirls are shown as risking all for Krishna, as loving him above all else but none is singled out for mention and none emerges as a rival. In this long account of Krishna's life what is overwhelmingly significant is that the name of his supreme cowgirl love is altogether omitted.

V

THE KRISHNA OF POETRY

(i) *The Triumph of Radha*

During the next two hundred years, from the tenth to the twelfth century, the Krishna story completely alters. It is not that the facts as given in the *Bhagavata Purana* are disputed. It is rather that the emphasis and view-point are changed. Krishna the prince and his consort Rukmini are relegated to the background and Krishna the cowherd lover brought sharply to the fore. Krishna is no longer regarded as having been born solely to kill a tyrant and rid the world of demons. His chief function now is to vindicate passion as the symbol of final union with God. We have already seen that to Indians this final union was the sole purpose of life and only one experience was at all comparable to it. It was the mutual ecstasy of impassioned lovers. 'In the embrace of his beloved, a man forgets the whole world—everything both within and without; in the same way, he who embraces the Self knows neither within nor without.'[1] The function of the new Krishna was to defend these two premises—that romantic love was the most exalted experience in life and secondly, that of all the roads to salvation, the impassioned adoration of God was the one most valid. God must be adored. Krishna himself was God and since he had shown divine love in passionately possessing the cowgirls, he was best adored by recalling these very encounters. As a result, Krishna's relations with the cowgirls were now enormously magnified and as part of this fresh appraisal, a particular married cowgirl, Radha, enters the story as the enchanting object of his passions. We have seen how on one occasion in the *Bhagavata Purana*, Krishna disappears taking with him a single girl, how they then make love together in a forest bower and how when the girl tires and begs Krishna to carry her, he abruptly leaves her. The girl's name is not mentioned but enough is said to suggest that she is Krishna's favourite. This hint is now developed. Radha, for this is the girl's name, is recognized as the loveliest of all the cowgirls. She is the daughter of the cowherd Vrishabhanu and his wife, Kamalavati, and is married to Ayana, a brother of Yasoda. Like

[1] Note 15.

other cowgirls, her love for Krishna is all-consuming and compels her to ignore her family honour and disregard her husband. Krishna, for his part, regards her as his first love. In place, therefore, of courtly adventures and battles with demons, Krishna's adulterous romance is now presented as all in all.[1] It is the moods, feelings and emotions of a great love-affair which are the essence of the story and this, in turn, is to serve as a sublime allegory expressing and affirming the love of God for the soul. With this dramatic revolution in the story, we begin to approach the Krishna of Indian painting.

Such a change can hardly have come about without historical reasons and although the exact circumstances must perhaps remain obscure, we can see in this sharp reversal of roles a clear response to certain Indian needs. From early times, romantic love had been keenly valued, Sanskrit poets such as Kalidasa, Amaru and Bhartrihari celebrating the charms of womanly physique and the raptures of sex. What, in fact, in other cultures had been viewed with suspicion or disquiet was here invested with nobility and grandeur. Although fidelity had been demanded in marriage, romantic liaisons had not been entirely excluded and thus there was a sense in which the love-poetry of the early Indian middle ages had been partly paralleled by actual courtly or village practice. From the tenth century onwards, however, a tightening of domestic morals had set in, a tightening which was further intensified by the Muslim invasions of the twelfth and thirteen centuries. Romance as an actual experience became more difficult of attainment and this was exacerbated by standard views of marriage. In early India, marriage had been regarded as a contract between families and romantic love between husband and wife as an accidental, even an unexpected product of what was basically a utilitarian agreement. With the seclusion of women and the laying of even greater stress on wifely chastity, romantic love was increasingly denied. Yet the need for romance remained and we can see in the prevalence of love-poetry a substitute for wishes repressed in actual life.[2] It is precisely this role which the story of Krishna the cowherd lover now came to perform. Krishna, being God, had been beyond morals and hence had practised conduct which, if indulged in by men, might well have been wrong. He had given practical expression to romantic longings and had behaved with all the passionate freedom normally stifled by social duty, conjugal ethics and family morals. From this point of view, Krishna the prince was a mere pillar of boring respectability. Nothing in his conduct could arouse delight for

[1] Note 16.   [2] Note 17.

everything he did was correct and proper. Krishna the cowherd on the other hand, was spontaneous, irresponsible and free. His love for the cowgirls had had a lively freedom. The love between them was nothing if not voluntary. His whole life among the cowherds was simple, natural and pleasing and as their rapturous lover nothing was more obvious than that the cowgirls should adore him. In dwelling, then, on Krishna, it was natural that the worshipper should tend to disregard the prince and should concentrate instead on the cowherd. The prince had revered Brahmans and supported established institutions. The cowherd had shamed the Brahmans of Mathura and discredited ceremonies and festivals. He had loved and been loved and in his contemplation lay nothing but joy. The loves of Krishna, in fact, were an intimate fulfilment of Indian desires, an exact sublimation of intense romantic needs and while other factors must certainly have played their part, this is perhaps the chief reason why, at this juncture, they now enchanted village and courtly India.

The results of this new approach are apparent in two distinct ways. The *Bhagavata Purana* continues to be the chief chronicle of Krishna's acts but the last half of Book Ten and all of Book Eleven fall into neglect.[1] In their place, the story of Krishna's relations with the cowgirls is given new poignancy and precision. Radha is constantly mentioned and in all the incidents in the *Purana* involving cowgirls, it is she who is given pride of place. At the river Jumna, when Krishna removes the cowgirls' clothes, Radha begs him to restore them. At the circular dance in which he joins with all the cowgirls, Radha receives his first attentions, dancing with him in the centre. When Krishna is about to leave for Mathura, it is Radha who heads the cowgirls and strives to detain him. She serves, in fact, as a symbol of all the cowgirls' love. At the same time, she is very far from being merely their spokesman or leader and while the later texts dwell constantly on her rapturous love-making with Krishna, they also describe her jealousy when Krishna makes love to other girls. Indeed the essence of their romance is that it includes a temporary estrangement and only after Krishna has neglected Radha, flirted with other cowgirls and then returned to her is their understanding complete.

The second result is the allegorical interpretation which Krishna's romances now received. In Christian literature, the longing of the soul for God was occasionally expressed in terms of sexual imagery —the works of the Spanish mystic, St. John of the Cross, including

[1] I.e. the whole of Krishna's career after his destruction of the tyrant.

'songs of the soul in rapture at having arrived at the height of perfection which is union with God.'

> Oh night that was my guide!
> Oh darkness dearer than the morning's pride,
> Oh night that joined the lover
> To the beloved bride
> Transfiguring them each into the other.
>
> Within my flowering breast
> Which only for himself entire I save
> He sank into his rest
> And all my gifts I gave
> Lulled by the airs with which the cedars wave.[1]

This same approach was now to clarify Radha's romance with Krishna. Radha, it was held, was the soul while Krishna was God. Radha's sexual passion for Krishna symbolized the soul's intense longing and her willingness to commit adultery expressed the utter priority which must be accorded to love for God. If ultimate union was symbolized by romantic love, then clearly nothing could approach such love in ultimate significance. In deserting their husbands and homes and wilfully committing adultery, Radha and the cowgirls were therefore illustrating a profound religious truth. Not only was their adultery proof of Krishna's charm, it was vital to the whole story. By worldly standards, they were committing the gravest of offences but they were doing it for Krishna who was God himself. They were therefore setting God above home and duty, they were leaving everything for love of God and in surrendering their honour, were providing the most potent symbol of what devotion meant. This approach explained other details. Krishna's flute was the call of God which caused the souls of men, the cowgirls, to forsake their worldly attachments and rush to love him. In removing the clothes of the cowgirls and requiring them to come before him naked, he was demonstrating the innocent purity with which the soul should wait on God. In himself neglecting Radha and toying with the cowgirls, he was proving, on one level, the power of worldly pleasures to seduce the soul but on another level, the power of God to love every soul irrespective of its character and status. From this point of view, the cowgirls were as much the souls of men as Radha herself and to demonstrate God's all-pervasive love, Krishna must therefore love not only Radha but every cowgirl. Equally, in the circular dance, by inducing every cowgirl to

[1] Roy Campbell, *The Poems of St. John of the Cross* (London, 1951), 11–12.

think that she and she alone was his partner, Krishna was proving how God is available to all. Finally it was realized that even those portions of the story which, at first sight, seemed cruel and callous were also susceptible of religious interpretation. When Radha has been loved in the forest and then is suddenly deserted, the reason is her pride—pride that because Krishna has loved her, she can assert herself by asking to be carried. Such assertiveness is incompatible with the kind of humble adoration necessary for communion with God. To prove this, therefore, Radha's pride must be destroyed and Krishna resorts to this seemingly brusque desertion. Action, in fact, which by human standards would be reprehensible is once again a means for imparting spiritual wisdom. In a similar way, Krishna's departure for Mathura and final abandonment of the cowgirls was accorded a religious interpretation. At one level, his departure symbolized 'the dark night of the soul,' the experience which comes to every devotee when, despite the most ardent longing, the vision fades. At another level, it illustrated how life must be lived when God or Vishnu was no longer on earth. If Krishna's love-making was intended to symbolize the ultimate rapture, his physical absence corresponded to conditions as they normally existed. In instructing the cowgirls to meditate upon him in their minds, Krishna was only attuning them to life as it must necessarily appear after he has left the human stage.

It was these conceptions which governed the cult of Krishna from the twelfth century onwards and, as we shall shortly see, informed the poems which were now to celebrate his love for Radha.

(ii) *The Gita Govinda*

The first poem to express this changed conception is the *Gita Govinda*—the Song of the Cowherd—a Sanskrit poem written by the Bengali poet, Jayadeva, towards the close of the twelfth century. Its subject is the estrangement of Radha and Krishna caused by Krishna's love for other cowgirls, Radha's anguish at Krishna's neglect and lastly the rapture which attends their final reunion. Jayadeva describes Radha's longing and Krishna's love-making with glowing sensuality yet the poem reverts continually to praise of Krishna as God.

> If in recalling Krishna to mind there is flavour
> Or if there is interest in love's art
> Then to this necklace of words—sweetness,
>   tenderness, brightness—
> The words of Jayadeva, listen.

He aims, in fact, at inducing 'recollection of Krishna in the minds of the good' and adds a description of the forest in springtime solely, he says, in order once again to recall Krishna.[1] When, at last, the poem has come triumphantly to its close, Jayadeva again exhorts people to adore Krishna and 'place him for ever in their hearts, Krishna the source of all merit.'

The poem begins with a preface of four lines describing how Krishna's romance with Radha first began. The sky, it says, was dark with clouds. All around lay the vast forest. Night was coming up and Nanda who had taken the youthful Krishna with him is alarmed lest in the gathering gloom the boy should get lost. Radha, who is somewhat older, is with them, so Nanda desires her to take Krishna home. Radha leads him away but as they wander by the river, passion mounts in their hearts. They forget that Nanda has told them to hurry home. Radha ignores the motherly character of her mission and loitering in the trees, the two commence their dalliance.[2] In this way the love of Radha and Krishna arises—the love which is to dominate their hearts with ever-growing fervour.

The poem then leaps a period of time and when the drama opens, a crisis has occurred. Radha, after long enjoying Krishna's passionate embraces, finds herself abruptly neglected. Charming but faithless, Krishna is now pursuing other girls and the jilted Radha wanders alone. Meanwhile spring has come to the forest and the thought that others are enjoying Krishna's love tortures her to the point of madness. As she broods on her lost joys, a friend describes to her what is happening.[3]

> Sandal and garment of yellow and lotus garlands upon his body of blue,
> In his dance the jewels of his ears in movement dangling over his smiling cheeks,
> Krishna here disports himself with charming women given to love.
> He embraces one woman, he kisses another, and fondles another beautiful one.
> He looks at another one lovely with smiles, and starts in pursuit of another woman.
> Krishna here disports himself with charming women given to love.[4]

Suddenly Radha sees Krishna[5] and going into the midst of the cowgirls, she kisses him violently and clasps him to her; but Krishna is so inflamed by the other girls that he abandons her in a thicket.

As Radha broods on his behaviour, she is filled with bitter sadness.[6]

[1] Note 18. [2] Plate 20. [3] Plates 21 and 22.
[4] Note 19. [5] Plate 23. [6] Plate 24.

Yet her love is still so strong that she cannot bring herself to blame him and instead calls to mind his charm.

> I remember Krishna, the jests he made, who placed his sport in the pastoral dance,
> The sweet of whose nectar of lips kept flowing with notes of his luring melodious flute,
> With the play of whose eyes and the toss of whose head the earrings kept dangling upon his cheeks.
>
> I remember Krishna, the jests he made, who placed his sport in the pastoral dance,
> Whose brow had a perfect sandal spot, as among dark clouds the disc of the moon,
> Whose door-like heart was without pity when crushing the bosoms of swelling breasts.
>
> Desire even now in my foolish mind for Krishna,
> For Krishna—without me—lusting still for the herd-girls.
> Seeing only the good in his nature, what shall I do?
> Agitated I feel no anger. Pleased without cause, I acquit him.

And she continues:

> O make him enjoy me, my friend, that Krishna so fickle,
> I who am shy like a girl on her way to the first of her trysts of love,
> He who is charming with flattering words, I who am tender
> In speech and smiling, he on whose hip the garment lies loosely worn.
>
> O make him enjoy me, my friend, that Krishna so fickle,
> Me who sweated and moistened all over my body with love's exertion,
> That Krishna whose cheeks were lovely with down all standing on end as he thrilled,
> Whose half-closed eyes were languid, and restless with brimming desire.
>
> O make him enjoy me, my friend, that Krishna so fickle,
> Me whose masses of curls were like loose-slipping flowers, whose amorous words
> Were vague as of doves, that Krishna whose bosom is marked
> With scratches, surpassing all in his love that the science of love could teach.
>
> O make him enjoy me, my friend, that Krishna so fickle,
> To whose act of desire accomplished the anklets upon my feet bejewelled
> Vibrated sounding, who gave his kisses seizing the hair of the head,
> And to whom in his passionate love my girdle sounded in eloquence sweet.

As Radha sits longing for him in lonely sadness, Krishna suddenly repents, is filled with remorse and abruptly goes in quest of her. He does not know, however, where to find her and as he wanders, he expresses his sorrow.

> Radha so deeply wronged, troubled to see me surrounded by women,
> She went, and I, in fear of my guilt, made no attempt to stop her,
> Alas, alas, she is gone in anger, her love destroyed.
>
> O my slender one, I imagine your heart is dejected,
> I cannot console you kneeling in homage, I know not where to find you.
> If you pardon me now I shall never repeat this neglect of you ever—
> O beautiful, give me your pleasure again. I burn with desire.

As Krishna searches unavailingly, Radha's friend lights upon him and conveys news of her love-tormented state.

> Armour she makes of tender lotus garlands to hide her bosom from you,
> Large garlands, as if to protect you from heavy showers of shafts from the god of love.
> She fears an attack of Love upon you, and lies away hidden;
> She wastes away, Krishna, parted from you.

As he hears this, Krishna is torn with longing. He does not, however, go immediately to Radha but instead asks the friend to bring Radha to him. The girl departs, meets Radha and gives her Krishna's message. She then describes Krishna's love-lorn state:

> When he hears the noise of swarms of bees, he covers his ears from their humming;
> Pain he feels, night after night, of a heart in love that is parted.
> He droops, separated from you, O friend, the wearer of garlands.

The girl assures Radha that Krishna is contrite and urges her to delay no longer.

> He has gone into the trysting place, full of all desired bliss, O you with lovely hips delay no more
> O go forth now and seek him out, him the master of your heart, him endowed with passion's lovely form.
>
> On fallen feathers of the birds, on leaves about the forest floor, he lies excited making there his bed,
> And he gazes out upon the path, looks about with trembling eyes, anxious, looking out for your approach.

> There on that bed of tender leaves, O lotus-eyed, embrace his hips,
>   his naked hips from whence the girdle drops,
> Those hips from whence the garment falls, those loins which are a
>   treasure heap, the fountain and the source of all delight.

Radha would willingly go but she is now so sick with love that she can no longer move. The girl has, therefore, to go once more to Krishna and describe Radha's state.

> In secret on every side she sees you
> Drinking the honied sweet of her lips.
> Where Radha stays now she wilts away,
> She may live no longer without your skill,
> Again and again she keeps telling her friend,
> 'O why must Krishna delay to come?'
>
> Of her jewels abundant her limbs she adorns and spreads out her
>   bed—
> Imagining you on her fluttering couch of leaves—
> And so to indulge, in a hundred ways, in the sport of love
> She is fully resolved, arranging her bed with every adornment;
> Not another night may that beautiful girl endure without you.
> Why so much apathy, Krishna, beside the fig tree?
> O brother, why not go to the pasture of eyes, the abode of bliss?

Despite this message, however, Krishna still delays and Radha, who has half expected him, endures still greater anguish.

> My lover has failed to come to the trysting place,
> It is perhaps that his mind is dazed, or perhaps that he went to another
>   woman
> Or lured perhaps by festive folk, that he delays,
> Or perhaps along the dark fringe of the forest he wanders lost.

She imagines him toying with another cowgirl.

> A certain girl, excelling in her charms unrivalled, dallies with the
>   sportive Krishna
> Her face, a moon, is fondled by the fluttering petals in her hair,
> The exciting moisture of his lips induces langour in her limbs,
> Her earrings bruise her cheeks while dancing with the motion of her
>   head,
> Her girdle by the tremor of her moving hips is made to tinkle,
> She utters senseless sounds, through fever of her love,
> He decorates with crimson flowers her curly tresses, curls which are
>   upon her lively face a mass of clouds,
> Flowers with crimson flashings lovely in the forest of her tresses, haunt
>   of that wild creature love's desire.

And thinking of her own hapless state, Radha contrasts it bitterly with that of the fortunate girl.

> She who with the wearer of the garland lies in dalliance,
> With him whose lovely mouth is like a lotus that is opening,
> With him whose words are nectar in their sweetness and their tenderness,
> With him who wears a garment streaked with gold, all white and beautiful
> Not made to sigh is she, my friend, derided by her girls!

Next morning Radha is standing with her girls when Krishna tries to approach her. Now, however, he has come too late. Radha has suffered too greatly. Her patience is at an end and although Krishna implores her to forgive him, she rounds on him in anger, ordering him to return to the other girl whom he has just left.[1]

> Your mouth, O Krishna, darkened, enhances the crimson beauty of your lovely body,
> Enhances with a darkness, a blackness that arises from the kissing of eyes coloured with black unguent.
> Go, Krishna, go. Desist from uttering these deceitful words.
> Follow her, you lotus-eyed, she who can dispel your trouble, go to her.
> I who follow you devoted—how can you deceive me, so tortured by love's fever as I am?
> O Krishna, like the look of you, your body which appears so black, that heart of yours a blackness shall assume.
> Follow her, you lotus-eyed, she who can dispel your trouble, go to her.

Faced with these reproaches, Krishna slinks away. Radha's friend knows, however, that despite her bitter anger, Radha desires nothing more than his love. She attempts, therefore, to instil in her a calmer frame of mind, urging her to end her pride and take Krishna back. She goes to look for Krishna and while she is absent, Krishna returns. Standing before Radha, he implores her once again to end her anger.

> If you speak but a little the moon-like gleam of your teeth will destroy the darkness frightful, so very terrible, come over me;
> Your moon of a face which glitters upon my eye, the moon-bird's eye, now makes me long for the sweet of your lips.
> O loved one, O beautiful, give up that baseless pride against me,
> My heart is burnt by the fire of longing; give me that drink so sweet of your lotus face.

[1] Plate 25.

> O you with beautiful teeth, if you are in anger against me, strike me then with your finger nails, sharp and like arrows,
> Bind me, entwining, with the cords of your arms, and bite me then with your teeth, and feel happy punishing.
> O loved one, O beautiful, give up that baseless pride against me.

At these words, Radha's anger leaves her; and when Krishna withdraws, it is to go to the forest and await her coming. Radha's joy returns. She decks herself in the loveliest of her ornaments and then, accompanied by her maids, moves slowly to the tryst.[1] As they reach the bower which Krishna has constructed, her friend urges her to enter.

> O you who bear on your face the smile that comes of the ardour of passion
> Sport with him whose love-abode is the floor of the beautiful bower.

Radha approaches and their love strains to its height.

> She looked at Krishna who desired only her, on him who for long wanted dalliance,
> Whose face with his pleasure was overwhelmed and who was possessed with desire
> After embracing her long and ardently, Krishna with his necklace of pearls
> Krishna like the Jumna in a mighty flood with its necklace of specks of foam.[2]

The cowgirls go and Krishna speaks to Radha.

> O woman with desire, place on this patch of flower-strewn floor your lotus foot,
> And let your foot through beauty win,
> To me who am the Lord of All, O be attached, now always yours.
> O follow me, my little Radha.
>
> O lovely woman, give me now the nectar of your lips, infuse new life into this slave of yours, so dead,
> This slave, whose heart is placed in you, whose body burned in separation, this slave denied the pleasure of your love.

Radha yields and as the night passes they achieve height upon height of sexual bliss.

> Their love play grown great was very delightful, the love play where thrills were a hindrance to firm embraces,

[1] Plate 26.   [2] Plate 27.

Where their helpless closing of eyes was a hindrance to longing looks at each other, and their secret talk to their drinking of each the other's nectar of lips, and where the skill of their love was hindered by boundless delight.

She loved as never before throughout the course of the conflict of love, to win, lying over his beautiful body, to triumph over her lover;
And so through taking the active part her thighs grew lifeless, and languid her vine-like arms, and her heart beat fast, and her eyes grew heavy and closed.

In the morning most wondrous, the heart of her lord was smitten with arrows of Love, arrows which went through his eyes,
Arrows which were her nailed-scratched bosom, her reddened sleep-denied eyes, her crimson lips from a bath of kisses, her hair disarranged with the flowers awry, and her girdle all loose and slipping.
With hair knot loosened and stray locks waving, her cheeks perspiring, her glitter of lips impaired,
And the necklace of pearls not appearing fair because of her jar-shaped breast being denuded,
And her belt, her glittering girdle, dimmed in beauty,
The happy one drank of the face where the lips were washed with the juice of his mouth,
His mouth half open uttering amorous noises, vague and delirious, the rows of teeth in the breath of an indrawn sigh delightedly chattering.
Drank of the face of that deer-eyed woman whose body lay helpless, released of excessive delight, the thrilling delight of embraces.

When their passion is at last ended, Radha begs Krishna to help her with her toilet.

She said to the joy of her heart,
Adorn the curl on my brow which puts the lotus to shame, my spotless brow,
Make a beautiful spot on my forehead, a spot with the paste of the sandal,
O giver of pride, on my tresses, untidy now on account of desire, place flowers,
Place on my hips the girdle, the clothes and the jewels,
Cover my beautiful loins, luscious and firm, the cavern of Love to be feared.
Make a pattern upon my breasts and a picture on my cheeks and fasten over my loins a girdle,
Bind my masses of hair with a beautiful garland and place many bracelets upon my hands and jewelled anklets upon my feet.

Krishna does so and with a final celebration of Krishna as God and of the song itself—its words 'sweeter than sugar, like love's own glorious flavour'—the poem ends.

(iii) *Later Poetry*

Jayadeva's poem quickly achieved renown in Northern and Western India and from the early thirteenth century became a leading model for all poets who were enthralled by Krishna as God and lover. In Western India, Bilvamangala, a poet of Malabar, composed a whole galaxy of Krishna songs, his poem, the *Balagopala Stuti* (The Childhood of Krishna) earning for him the title 'the Jayadeva of the South.' But it is during the fifteenth and sixteenth centuries that the most important developments occurred. In Bengal, the poets Vidyapati and Chandi Das flourished in about the year 1420, while in Western India, Mira Bai, a local princess, began a wide-spread popular movement. Mira Bai was followed by Vallabhacharya (born 1478) who in turn inspired four poet disciples—Krishna Das, Sur Das, Parmanand Das and Kumbhan Das. All these were at their height in the middle of the sixteenth century, writing Hindi poems in which Radha's adventures with Krishna and their rapturous love-making were devotedly described.[1]

The work of Sur Das was of special importance for in one of his compositions he took each of the thirty-six traditional modes of Indian music—the *Ragas* and *Raginis*—but instead of celebrating them as separate 'musical characters,' appended to each a love-poem about Krishna. Sur Das was followed by Keshav Das of Orchha (fl. 1580), Govind Das (fl. 1590), Bihari Lal (fl. 1650) and Kali Das (fl. 1700)—all poets in whom religious ecstasy was blended with a feeling for passionate romance. Of these poets Bihari Lal is famous for the *Sat Sai* in which he celebrated Krishna's romance in seven hundred verses.

All this later poetry differed from the *Gita Govinda* in one important respect. Instead of dwelling on the temporary rupture in Radha and Krishna's relationship, it roved freely over the many phases of their love-making, subjecting every incident to delighted analysis. A poet thought and felt himself into Radha's mind when as a young girl about to become a woman she discovered for the first time the exquisite sensations of awakening love. Or he imagined he was Krishna stumbling on Radha by accident and being stirred to ecstasy by his first glimpse of her glowing charms. Sometimes he even became the unseen viewer of their rapturous exchanges,

[1] Plate 29.

comforting Radha with sage remarks or egging her on to appease her hungry lover. In this way many incidents not recorded of any cowgirl in the *Bhagavata Purana*, though possibly preserved in oral tradition, came gradually into prominence, thereby confirming Radha as Krishna's greatest love.

The following incidents will illustrate this process. Radha would be described as one day taking her curds and milk to a village the farther side of the river Jumma. Krishna hears of her expedition and along with other cowherd boys waylays Radha and her friends and claims a toll. Radha refuses to pay but at last offers to make a token gift provided he ferries them over. Meanwhile a cowherd boy has hidden the boat and night is coming on. It is now too late to return so the girls have no alternative but to stay with Krishna. They lie down by the bank but in the darkness give Krishna not only the toll but also their souls and bodies.

In another poem, Krishna is shown pestering the cowgirls for curds. Radha decides to stand this no longer and partly in jest dresses herself up as a constable. When Krishna next teases the girls, she descends upon him, catches him by the wrist and 'arrests' him as a thief.[1]

It is in the poems of Chandi Das, however, that Krishna's most daring ruses are described. Having once gained admittance to Radha's house by dressing himself as a cowgirl, he is shown pretending to be a flower-seller. He strings some flowers into a bunch of garlands, dangles them on his arm and strolls blandly down the village street. When he reaches Radha's house, he goes boldly in and is taken by Radha into a corner where she starts to bargain. Krishna asks her to let him first adorn her with a garland and then she can pay him. Radha agrees and as he slips a garland over her head, Krishna kisses her. Radha suddenly sees who it is and holds his hand.

On another occasion, Radha is ill from love and is lying at home on her bed. Krishna thereupon becomes a doctor and goes from house to house curing the sick. So successful are his cures that Radha also is tempted to consult the new doctor and sends a maid to call him. Krishna comes but before entering adopts a wild disguise—putting his clothes on inside out, matting his hair with mud, and slinging a bag of roots and plants over his shoulder. As he enters, he sits on Radha's bed, lifts her veil, gazes intently at her face and declares that certainly she is very ill indeed. He then takes her pulse and says, 'it is the water of love that is rotting her heart like

[1] Plate 35.

a poison.' Radha is elated at this diagnosis, rouses herself and stretches her limbs. 'You have understood my trouble,' she says. 'Now tell me what I am to do.' 'I feel somewhat diffident at explaining my remedy,' replies the doctor, 'But if I had the time and place, I could ease your fever and cure you utterly.' As he says this, Radha knows that he is Krishna and this is only another of his reckless wiles designed to bring him near her.

But it was less in the recording of new incidents than in lyrical descriptions of Radha and Krishna, their physical charms and ecstatic meetings, that the poets excelled.

i

Krishna is dancing in a medley of moods and poses.
His crown sways, his eye-brows move,
Displaying the arts of a clever dancer.
The swing of his waist makes his girdle sing
And the anklets jingle.
One fancies one is listening to the sweet voice of a pair of geese as they touch each other in dalliance.
The bangles glitter and the rings and armlets shoot their rays.
When with passion he moves his arms, what grace the movements bless!
Now he dances after the gait of ladies and now in a manner of his own.
The poet's lord is the jewel of the passionate
And builds his dance in the depths of ecstasy.[1]

(Sur Das)

ii

With Krishna in their midst the cowherds come to their homes.
The calves and cows are ahead, frisking and playing as they go.
All the pipes and horns go forth, each his own notes playing.
The sound of the flute moves the cows to low as they raise a cloud of dust.
The crown of peacocks' feathers glistens on the head like a young moon.
The cowherd boys frolic on the path and Krishna in the centre sings his song.
Ravished by the sight, the cowgirls pour out their minds and bodies,
Gazing on Krishna, quenching their heart's desire.

(Sur Das)

[1] Note 20.

iii

Radha's glances dart from side to side.
Her restless body and clothes are heavy with dust.
Her glistening smile shines again and again.
Shy, she raises her skirt to her lips.
Startled, she stirs and once again is calm,
As now she enters the ways of love.
Sometimes she gazes at her blossoming breasts
Hiding them quickly, then forgetting they are there.
Childhood and girlhood melt in one
And young and old are both forgotten.
Says Vidyapati: O Lord of life,
Do you not know the signs of youth?[1]

(Vidyapati)

Each day the breasts of Radha swelled.
Her hips grew shapely, her waist more slender.
Love's secrets stole upon her eyes.
Startled her childhood sought escape.
Her plum-like breasts grew large,
Harder and crisper, aching for love.
Krishna soon saw her as she bathed
Her filmy dress still clinging to her breasts,
Her tangled tresses falling on her heart,
A golden image swathed in yak's tail plumes.
Says Vidyapati: O wonder of women,
Only a handsome man can long for her.

(Vidyapati)

v

There was a shudder in her whispering voice.
She was shy to frame her words.
What has happened tonight to lovely Radha?
Now she consents, now she is scared.
When asked for love, she closes up her eyes,
Eager to reach the ocean of desire.
He begs her for a kiss.
She turns her mouth away
And then, like a night lily, the moon seized her.
She felt his touch startling her girdle.
She knew her love treasure was being robbed.
With her dress she covered up her breasts.
The treasure was left uncovered.
Vidyapati wonders at the neglected bed.
Lovers are busy in each other's arms.

(Vidyapati)

[1] Note 20.

vi

Awake, Radha, awake
Calls the parrot and its love
For how long must you sleep,
Clasped to the heart of your Dark-stone?
Listen. The dawn has come
And the red shafts of the sun
Are making us shudder.

(Vidyapati)

vii

Startled, the parrot calls.
See those young lovers are still asleep.
On a bed of tender leaves
His dark figure is lying still.
She, the fair one,
Looks like a piece of jewelled gold.
They have emptied their quivers.
All their flower-arrows are discharged,
Drowning each other in the joy of love.
O lovely Radha, awake.
Your friends are going to the temple.
Asks Govind Das:
Whose business is it
To interrupt the ways of love?

(Govind Das)

In another kind of poem, Radha and Krishna are themselves made to speak—Krishna, for example, describing his first glimpses of Radha and Radha struggling to evoke in words the ecstasies of their love.

viii

Like stilled lightning her fair face.
I saw her by the river,
Her hair dressed with jasmine,
Plaited like a coiled snake.
O friend, I will tell you
The secret of my heart.
With her darting glances
And gentle smiles
She made me wild with love.
Throwing and catching a ball of flowers,
She showed me to the full
Her youthful form.

Uptilted breasts
Peeped from her dress.
Her face was bright
With taunting smiles.
With anklet bells
Her feet shone red.
Says Chandi Das:
Will you see her again?
(Chandi Das)

ix

Listen, O lovely darling,
Cease your anger.
I promise by the golden pitchers of your breasts
And by your necklace-snake,
Which now I gather in my hands,
If ever I touch anyone but you
May your necklace-snake bite me;
And if my words do not ring true,
Punish me as I deserve.
Bind me in your arms, hit me with your thighs,
Choke my heart with your milk-swollen breasts,
Lock me day and night in the prison of your heart.
(Vidyapati)

x

Never have I seen such love nor heard of it.
Even the eyelids' flutter
Holds eternity.
Clasped to my breasts, you are far from me.
I would keep you as a veil close to my face.
I shudder with fright when you turn your eyes away,
As one body, we spend the night,
Sinking in the deeps of delight.
As dawn comes, we see with anxious hearts
Life desert us.
The very thought breaks my heart.
Says Chandi Das:
O sweet girl, how I understand.
(Chandi Das)

xi

O friend, I cannot tell you
Whether he was near or far, real or a dream.
Like a vine of lightning,
As I chained the dark one,
I felt a river flooding in my heart.

> Like a shining moon,
> I devoured that liquid face.
> I felt stars shooting around me.
> The sky fell with my dress
> Leaving my ravished breasts.
> I was rocking like the earth.
> In my storming breath
> I could hear my ankle-bells,
> Sounding like bees.
> Drowned in the last-waters of dissolution
> I knew that this was not the end.
> Says Vidyapati:
> How can I possibly believe such nonsense?
>
> (Vidyapati)

(iv) *The Rasika Priya*

It is a third development, however, which reveals the insistent attractions of Krishna the divine lover. From about the seventh century onwards Indian thinkers had been fascinated by the great variety of possible romantic experiences. Writers had classified feminine beauty and codified the different situations which might arise in the course of a romance. A woman, for example, would be catalogued according as she was 'one's own, another's or anyone's' and whether she was young, adolescent or adult. Beauties with adult physiques were divided into unmarried and married, while cutting across such divisions was yet another based on the particular circumstances in which a woman might find herself. Such circumstances were normally eight in number—when her husband or lover was on the point of coming and she was ready to receive him; when she was parted from him and was filled with longing; when he was constant and she was thus enjoying the calm happiness of stable love; when, for the time being, she was estranged due to some quarrel or tiff; when she had been deceived; when she had gone to meet her lover but had waited in vain, thereby being jilted; when her husband or lover had gone abroad and she was faced with days of lonely waiting; and finally, when she had left the house and gone to meet him. Ladies in situations such as these were known as *nayikas* and the text embodying the standard classification was the Sanskrit treatise, the *Bharatiya Natya Sastra*. A similar analysis was made of men—lovers or *nayakas* being sometimes divided into fourteen different types.

Until the fourteenth century, such writings were studies in erotics rather than in literature—the actual situations rather than their literary treatment being the authors' prime concern. During the fourteenth century, however, questions of literary taste began to be discussed and there arose a new type of Sanskrit treatise, showing how different kinds of lover should be treated in poetry and illustrating the correct attitudes by carefully chosen verses. In all these writings the standard of reference was human passion. The lovers of poetry might bear only a slight relation to lovers in real life. Many of the situations envisaged might rarely, if ever, occur. It was sufficient that granted some favourable accident, some chance suspension of normal circumstances, lovers could be imagined as acting in these special ways.

It is out of this critical literature that our new development springs. As vernacular languages were used for poetry, problems of Hindi composition began to dwarf those of Sanskrit. It was necessary to discuss how best to treat each *nayika* and *nayaka* not only in Sanskrit but in Hindi poetry also, and to meet this situation Keshav Das, the poet of Orchha in Bundelkhand, produced in 1591 his *Rasika Priya*. Here all the standard situations were once again examined, *nayikas* and *nayakas* were newly distinguished and verses illustrating their appropriate treatments were systematically included. The book differed, however, in two important ways from any of its predecessors. It was written in Hindi, Keshav Das himself supplying both poems and commentary and what was even more significant, the *nayaka* or lover was portrayed not as any ordinary well-bred young man but as Krishna himself.[1] As a girl waits at the tryst it is not for an ordinary lover but for Krishna that Keshav Das depicts her as longing.

'Is he detained by work? Is he loath to leave his friends? Has he had a quarrel? Is his body uneasy? Is he afraid when he sees the rainy dark? O Krishna, Giver of Bliss, why do you not come?'[2]

As a girl waits by her bed looking out through her door, it is the prospect of Krishna's arrival—not of an ordinary lover's—that makes her happy.

'As she runs, her blue dress hides her limbs. She hears the wind ruffling the trees and the birds shifting in the night. She thinks it must be he. How she longs for love, watching for Krishna like a bird in a cage.'

When the lover arrives at dawn, having failed to come in the night, the girl (another *nayika*, 'one who has been deceived') upbraids

[1] Plate 28.   [2] Note 21.

Krishna for wandering about like a crow, picking up worthless grains of rice, wasting his hours in bad company and ruining houses by squatting in them like an owl.

Similarly when a married girl sits longing for her husband's return, her companion comments not on an ordinary husband's conduct but on that of Krishna. 'He said he would not be long. "I shall be back," he said, "as soon as I have had my meal." But now it is hours since he went. Why does he sit beside them and no one urge him to go? Does he know that her eyes are wet with tears, that she is crying her heart out because he does not come?'

Krishna, in fact, is here regarded as resuming in himself all possible romantic experiences. He is no longer merely the cowherd lover or the hero prince, the central figure of a sacred narrative. Neither is he merely or only the lover of Radha. He is deemed to know love from every angle and thus to sanctify all modes of passionate behaviour. He is love itself.

Such a development concludes the varied phases through which the character of Krishna has passed. The cowherd lover supersedes the hero prince. Radha becomes all in all, yet touches of Krishna's princely majesty remain throughout. Even as a cowherd Krishna shows an elegance and poise which betrays his different origin. And in the *Rasika Priya* it is once again his courtly aura which determines his new role. A blend of prince and cowherd, Krishna ousts from poetry the courtly lovers who previously had seemed the acme of romance. Adoration of God acquires the grace and charm of courtly loving, passionate sensuality all the refinement and nobility of a spiritual religion. It is out of all these varied texts that the Krishna of Indian painting now emerges.

VI

THE KRISHNA OF PAINTING

Indian pictures of Krishna confront us with a series of difficult problems. The most exalted expressions of the theme are mainly from Kangra, a large Hindu state within the Punjab Hills.[1] It was here that Krishna, the cowherd lover, was most fully celebrated. Pictures were produced in large numbers and the Kangra style with its delicate refinement exactly mirrored the enraptured poetry of the later cult. This painting was due entirely to a particular Kangra ruler, Raja Sansar Chand (1775-1823)—his delight in painting causing him to spare no cost in re-creating the Krishna idyll in exquisite terms. Elsewhere, however, conditions varied. At the end of the sixteenth century, it was not a Hindu but a Muslim ruler who commissioned the greatest illustrations of the story. In the seventeenth and eighteenth centuries, Hindu patrons were the rule but in certain states it was junior members of the ruling family rather than the Raja himself who worshipped Krishna. Sometimes it was not the ruling family but members of the merchant community who sponsored the artists and, occasionally, it was even a pious lady or devout princess who served as patron. Such differences of stimulus had vital effects and, as a consequence, while the cult of Krishna came increasingly to enthrall the northern half of India, its expression in art was the reverse of neat and orderly. Where a patron was so imbued with love for Krishna that adoration of the cowherd lover preceded all, the intensity of his feeling itself evoked a new style. There then resulted the Indian equivalent of pictures by El Greco, Grunewald or Altdorfer—paintings in which the artist's own religious emotions were the direct occasion of a new manner. In other cases, the patron might adhere to Krishna, pay him nominal respect or take a moderate pleasure in his story but not evince a burning enthusiasm. In such cases, paintings of Krishna would still be produced but the style would merely repeat existing conventions. The pictures which resulted would then resemble German paintings of the Danube or Cologne schools—pictures in which the artist applied an already mature style to a religious theme but did not originate a fresh mode of expression. Whether the

[1] Plates 3, 5, 6, 8, 9, 11, 13-17, 21 and 36.

greatest art resulted from the first or second method was problematical for the outcome depended as much on the nature of the styles as on the artist's powers. In considering Indian pictures of Krishna, then, we must be prepared for sudden fluctuations in expression and abrupt differences of style and quality. Adoration of Krishna was to prove one of the most vital elements in village and courtly life. It was to capture the imagination of Rajput princes and to lead to some of the most intimate revelations of the Indian mind. Yet in art its expression was to hover between the crude and the sensitive, the savage and the exquisite. It was to stimulate some of the most delicate Indian pictures ever painted and, at the same time, some of the most forceful.

The first pictures of Krishna to be painted in India fall within this second category. In about 1450, one version of the *Gita Govinda* and two of the *Balagopala Stuti* were produced in Western India.[1] They were doubtless made for middle-class patrons and were executed in Western India for one important reason. Dwarka, the scene of Krishna's life as a prince, and Prabhasa, the scene of the final slaughter, were both in Western India. Both had already become centres of pilgrimage and although Jayadeva had written his great poem far to the East, on the other side of India, pilgrims had brought copies with them while journeying from Bengal on visits to the sites. The *Gita Govinda* of Jayadeva had become in fact as much a Western Indian text as the *Balagopala Stuti* of Bilvamangala. With manuscript illustrations being already produced in Western India—but not, so far as we know, elsewhere— it was not unnatural that the first illustrated versions of these poems should be painted here. And it is these circumstances which determined their style. Until the fifteenth century the chief manuscripts illustrated in Western India were Jain scriptures commissioned by members of the merchant community. Jainism had originated in the sixth century B.C. as a parallel movement to Buddhism. It had proved more accommodating to Hinduism, and when Buddhism had collapsed in Western India in the ninth century A.D., Jainism had continued as a local variant of Hinduism proper. Jain manuscripts had at first consisted of long rectangular strips made of palm-leaves on which the scriptures were written in heavy black letters. Each slip was roughly three inches wide and ten long and into the text had been inserted lean diagrammatic paintings either portraying Mahavira, the founder of the cult, or illustrating episodes in his earthly career.

[1] M. R. Mazumdar, 'The Gujarati School of Painting,' *Journal of the Indian Society of Oriental Art*, 1942, Vol. X, plates 3 and 4.

About 1400, palm-leaf was superseded by paper and from then onwards manuscripts were given slightly larger pages. Owing partly to their association with the same religious order and partly to their constant duplication, Jain manuscripts had early conformed to a certain rigid type. The painting was marked by lean and wiry outlines, brilliant red and blue and above all by an air of savage ferocity expressed through the idiom of faces shown three-quarter view with the farther eye detached and projecting into space. This style was exercised almost exclusively on Jain subjects and in the year 1400 it was the main style of painting in Western India and Rajasthan.

During the fifteenth century, this exclusive character gradually weakened. There arose the idea that besides Jain scriptures, secular poetry might also be illustrated and along with the growing devotion to Krishna as God came the demand for illustrated versions of Krishna texts. The three texts we have just mentioned are due to this tendency. All three are illustrated in the prevailing Jain style with its spiky angular idioms and all three have the same somewhat sinister air of barbarous frenzy. At the same time, all disclose a partial loosening of the rigid wiry convention, a more boisterous rhythm and a slightly softer treatment of trees and animals; and, although no very close correlation is possible, the theme itself may well have helped to precipitate these important changes.

Between 1450 and 1575, Western Indian painting continued to focus on Jain themes, adulterated to only a very slight extent by subjects drawn from poetry. It is possible that the Krishna story was also illustrated, but no examples have survived; and it is not until the very end of the sixteenth century that the Krishna theme again appears in painting and then in two distinct forms. The first is represented by a group of three manuscripts—two of them dated respectively 1598[1] and 1610[2] and consisting of the tenth book of the *Bhagavata Purana*, the third being yet another illustration of the *Gita Govinda*.[3] All three sets of illustrations are in a closely similar style—a style which, while possessing roots in Jain painting is now considerably laxer and more sprawling. The faces are no longer shown three-quarter view, the detached obtruding eye has gone and in place of the early sharpness there is now a certain

[1] Collection Maharaja of Jaipur, Pothikhana, Jaipur.
[2] Collection Maharaja of Jodhpur, Pustakaprakash, Jodhpur Fort.
[3] Plate 22. Collection N. C. Mehta, Bombay. For reproductions of 2 and 3, see Karl Khandalavala, 'Leaves from Rajasthan,' *Marg*, Vol. IV, No. 3. Figs. 8 and 10.

slovenly crudity. We do not know for whom these manuscripts were made nor even in what particular part of Western India or Rajasthan they were executed. They were clearly not produced in any great centre of painting and can hardly have been commissioned by a prince or merchant of much aesthetic sensibility. They prove, however, that a demand for illustrated versions of the Krishna story was persisting and suggest that even prosperous traders may perhaps have acted as patrons.

The second type is obviously the product of far more sophisticated influences. It is once again a copy of the *Gita Govinda* and was probably executed in about 1590 in or near Jaunpur in Eastern India. As early as 1465, a manuscript of the leading Jain scripture, the *Kalpasutra*, had been executed at Jaunpur for a wealthy merchant.[1] Its style was basically Western Indian, yet being executed in an area so far to the east, it also possessed certain novelties of manner. The heads were more squarely shaped, the eyes larger in proportion to the face, the ladies' drapery fanning out in great angular swirls. The bodies' contours were also delineated with exquisitely sharp precision. The court at the time was that of Hussain Shah, a member of the marauding Muslim dynasties which since the twelfth century had enveloped Northern India; and it is possibly due to persistent Muslim influence that painting revived in the last two decades of the sixteenth century. Illustrated versions of passionate love poetry were executed[2] and as part of the same vogue for poetic romance, the *Gita Govinda* may once again have been illustrated.[3] Between the style of these later pictures and that of the Jain text of 1465, there are such clear affinities that the same local tradition is obviously responsible. Yet the new group of paintings has a distinctive elegance all its own. As in the previous group, the detached projecting eye has gone. Each situation is treated with a slashing boldness. There is no longer a sense of cramping detail and the flat red backgrounds of Western Indian painting infuse the settings with hot passion. But it is the treatment of the feminine form which charges the pictures with sophisticated charm. The large breasts, the sweeping dip in the back, the proud curve of the haunches, the agitated jutting-out of the skirts, all these convey an air of vivid sensual charm. That Radha and Krishna should be portrayed in so civilized a manner is evidence of the power

[1] Moti Chandra, *Jain Miniature Paintings from Western India* (Ahmedabad, 1949), Figs. 99–105.
[2] Khandalavala, op. cit., Fig. 14; *The Art of India and Pakistan*, Pls. 81 and 82.
[3] Plates 23 and 24.

which the Krishna story had come to exercise on courtly minds. Krishna is portrayed not as God but as the most elegant of lovers, Radha and the cowgirls as the very embodiment of fashionable women.

Jaunpur painting does not seem to have survived the sixteenth century and for our next illustrations of the theme, we must turn to the school of painting fostered by the Mughals. During the sixteenth century at least three Muslim states other than Jaunpur itself had possessed schools of painting—Malwa in Central India and Bijapur and Ahmadnagar in the Deccan. Their styles can best be regarded as Indian offshoots of a Persian mode of painting which was current in the Persian province of Shiraz in about the year 1500. In this style, known as Turkman, the flat figures of previous Persian painting were set in landscapes of rich and glowing herbage, plants and trees being rendered with wild and primitive vigour. In each case the style was probably brought to India by Persian artists who communicated it to Indian painters or themselves adjusted it to local conditions. And it is this process which was repeated but on an altogether grander scale by the Muslim dynasty of the Mughals. Under the emperor Akbar (1556–1605), the Mughals absorbed the greater part of Northern India, concentrating in one imperial court more power and wealth than had probably been amassed at any previous time in India. Among Akbar's cultural institutions was a great imperial library for which a colony of artists was employed in illustrating manuscripts in Persian. The founders of this colony were Persian and it is once again a local style of Persian painting which forms the starting point. This style is no longer the Turkman style of Shiraz but a later style—a local version of Safavid painting as current in Khurasan. With its lively and delicate naturalism it not only corresponded to certain predilections of the emperor Akbar himself, but seems also to have appealed to Indian artists recruited to the colony. Its representational finesse made it an ideal medium for transcribing the Indian scene and the appearance at the court of European miniatures, themselves highly naturalistic, stimulated this character still further. The result was the sudden rise in India, between 1570 and 1605, of a huge new school of painting, exquisitely representational in manner and committed to a new kind of Indian naturalism. Such a school, the creation of an alien Muslim dynasty, would at first sight seem unlikely to produce illustrations of Hindu religion. Its main function was to illustrate works of literature, science and contemporary history—a function which resulted in such grandiose productions as the *Akbarnama* or Annals of Akbar, now preserved in the Victoria and Albert Museum.[1] None the less there are two ways in which Mughal painting, as developed under Akbar, contributed to the Krishna story. Akbar, although a Muslim by birth, was keenly interested in all religions and in his dealings with the Rajputs had shown himself markedly tolerant. He desired to minimise the hatred of Muslims for Hindus and believing it to arise from mutual ignorance, ordained that certain Hindu texts should be translated into Persian and thus rendered more accessible. The texts chosen were the two epics, the *Ramayana* and the *Mahabharata*, and of these Persian abridgements were duly prepared. The abridgement of the *Mahabharata*, known as the *Razmnama*, was probably completed in 1588 but illustrated copies, including the great folios now in the palace library at Jaipur, were probably not completed before 1595. As part of the project, its appendix, the *Harivansa* was also summarized and a separate volume with fourteen illustrations all concerned with Krishna is part of the great version now at Jaipur.[2] In these illustrations, it is Krishna the prince who is chiefly shown, all the pictures illustrating his career after he has left the cowherds. There is no attempt to stress his romantic qualities or to present him as a lover. He appears rather as the great fighter, the slayer of demons. Such a portrayal is what we might perhaps expect from a Mughal edition. None the less the paintings are remarkable interpretations, investing Krishna with an air of effortless composure, and exalting his princely grace. The style is notable for its use of smoothly flowing outlines and gentle shading, and although there is no direct connection, it is these characteristics which were later to be embodied in the Hindu art of the Punjab Hills.

Such interest by the Emperor may well have spurred Hindu members of the court to have other texts illustrated for, ten to fifteen years later, in perhaps 1615, a manuscript of the *Gita Govinda* was produced, its illustrations possessing a certain fairy-like refinement.[3] Krishna in a flowing dhoti wanders in meadows gay with feathered trees while Radha and her confidante appear in Mughal garb. Romance is hardly evident for it is the scene itself with its rustic prettiness which is chiefly stressed. Yet the patron by whom this version was commissioned may well have felt that it was sensitively

[1] For reproductions, see E. Wellesz, *Akbar's Religious Thought reflected in Mogul Painting* (London, 1952), Pls. 1-37.

[2] Reproduced Hendley, *Memorials, The Razm Namah*; see also Plates 1 and 2 below.

[3] *The Art of India and Pakistan*, Plate 88.

rendered and within its minor compass expressed to some extent the magical enchantment distilled by the verses. That the Emperor's stimulus survived his death is plain; for in about the year 1620, two manuscripts of the *Bhagavata Purana* appeared—both in a style of awkward crudity in which the idioms of Akbar's school of artists were consciously aped.[1] The manuscripts in question are at Bikaner and it is possible that one or two inferior Mughal artists, deprived of work at the central court, travelled out to this northerly Rajput state, daring the desert, and there produced these vapid works. It is likely that in the early years of the seventeenth century, many areas of India possessed no artists whatsoever and if a Hindu ruler was to copy Mughal fashion, the only artists available to him might be those of an inferior rank. And although exact data are wanting, such circumstances may well explain another document of Krishna, the first illustrated version of Keshav Das's *Rasika Priya*.[2] As we have seen, this poem was composed at Orchha in Bundelkhand in 1591, at a time when both poet and court were in close association with Akbar. Yet the version in question shows the same poverty-stricken manner with its crude aping of imperial idioms and utter lack of sensitive expression. There is no evidence that at this time Bundelkhand possessed its own school of painting and in consequence the most likely explanation is that yet another inferior artist trained in the early Mughal manner, migrated to the court and there produced this crude prosaic version. In none of these provincial Mughal pictures is there any feeling for Krishna as God or even as a character. The figures have a wooden doll-like stiffness, parodying by their evident jerkiness the exquisite emotions intended by the poet and we can only assume that impressed by the imperial example minor rulers or nobles encouraged struggling practitioners but in an atmosphere far removed from that of the great emperor.

Such paintings in a broken-down Akbari manner characterize the period 1615 to 1630. From then onwards Mughal painting, as it developed under the emperor Shah Jahan, concentrated on more courtly themes. The early interest in dramatic action disappeared and the demand for costly manuscripts, sumptuously illustrated, withered up. Under Aurangzeb, tolerant understanding gave way to a vicious proselytism and it was only in remote centres such as Bikaner that later Mughal artists exercised their style on Krishna themes. It is significant that at Bikaner their leader was a Muslim, Ruknuddin, and that his chief work was a series of pic-

[1] H. Goetz, *The Art and Architecture of Bikaner State* (Oxford, 1950), Fig. 91.
[2] Coomaraswamy, *Boston Catalogue, VI, Mughal Painting*, Plates 8–19.

tures illustrating the *Rasika Priya*.[1] His figures have a shallow prettiness of manner, stamping them once again as products of a style which, in its earliest phases, was admirably suited to recording dramatic action but which had little relevance to either religion or romance. For these a more poetic and symbolic manner was necessary and such a style appeared in the city of Udaipur in the Rajput State of Mewar.

Painting at Udaipur is inseparably associated with the influence of two great rulers—Rana Jagat Singh (1628-1652) and Rana Raj Singh (1652-1681) As early as 1605 pictures had been produced at the State's former capital, Chawand—the artist being a Muhammadan named Nasiruddin. His style was obviously quite independent of any Mughal influence and it is rather to the separate tradition of painting which had grown up in Malwa that we must look for its salient qualities—a tensely rhythmical line, a flamboyant use of strong emphatic colours, vigorous simplifications and boldly primitive idioms for plants and trees. It is this style which thirty or forty years later comes to luxuriant maturity in a series of illustrations executed at Udaipur.[2] Although the artists responsible included a Muslim, Shahabaddin, and a Hindu, Manohar, it is the Krishna theme itself which seems to have evoked this marvellous efflorescence. Rana Jagat Singh was clearly a devout worshipper whose faithful adhesion to Rajput standards found exhilarating compensations in Krishna's role as lover. Keshav Das's *Rasika Priya* achieved the greatest popularity at his court—its blend of reverent devotion and ecstatic passion fulfilling some of the deepest Rajput needs. Between the years 1645 and 1660 there accordingly occurred a systematic production not only of pictures illustrating this great poetic text but of the various books in the *Bhagavata Purana* most closely connected with Krishna's career. Krishna is shown as a Rajput princeling dressed in fashionable garb, threading his way among the cowgirls, pursuing his amorous inclinations and practising with artless guile the seductive graces of a courtly lover. Each picture has a passionate intensity—its rich browns and reds, greens and blues endowing its characters with glowing fervour, while Krishna and the cowgirls, with their sharp robust forms and great intent eyes, display a brusque vitality and an eager rapturous vigour. A certain simplification of structure—each picture possessing one or more rectangular compartments—enhances this effect while the addition of swirling

[1] Goetz, op. cit., Figs. 78 and 93.
[2] Plate 29. See also B. Gray, *Treasures of Indian Miniatures from the Bikaner Palace Collection* (Oxford, 1951), Plate 6.

trees studded with flowers imbues each wild encounter with a surging vegetative rhythm. Krishna is no longer the tepid well-groomed youth of Mughal tradition, but a vigorous Rajput noble expressing with decorous vehemence all the violent longings denied expression by the Rajput moral code. Such pictures have a lyrical splendour, a certain wild elation quite distinct from previous Indian painting and we can only explain these new stylistic qualities by reference to the cult of Krishna himself. The realization that Krishna was adorable, that his practice of romantic love was a sublime revelation of Godhead and that in his worship lay release is the motive force behind these pictures and the result is a new style transcending in its rhythmical assurance and glowing ardour all previous achievements.

Such an outburst of painting could hardly leave other areas unaffected and in the closing quarter of the seventeenth century, not only Bundi, the Rajput State immediately adjoining Udaipur to the east, but Malwa, the wild hilly area farther south east, witnessed a renaissance of painting. At Bundi, the style was obviously a direct development from that of Udaipur itself—the idioms for human figures and faces as well as the glowing colours being clearly based on Udaipur originals. At the same time, a kind of sumptuous luxuriance, a predilection for greens and oranges in brilliant juxtaposition, a delight in natural profusion and the use of recessions, shading and round volumes give each picture a distinctive aura.[1] In Malwa, on the other hand, the earlier tradition seems to have undergone a new resuscitation. Following various wars in Middle India, the former Muslim kingdom had been divided into fiefs— some being awarded to Rajput nobles of loyalty and valour. The result was yet another style of painting—comparable in certain ways to that of Bundi and Udaipur yet markedly original in its total effect. In place of tightly geometrical compositions, Malwa artists preferred a more fluid grouping, their straining luxuriant trees blending with swaying creepers to create a soft meandering rhythm and only the human figures, with their sharply cut veils and taut intense faces, expressing the prevailing cult of frenzied passion.[2] Such schools of painting reflected the Rajput need for passionate romance rather than any specially strong adhesion to Krishna, the divine lover. Although one copy of the *Rasika Priya* and one of the *Bhagavata Purana* were executed at both these centres, their chief subjects were the *ragas* and *raginis* (the thirty-six modes

[1] Plates 28 and 32. See also Archer, *Indian Painting*, Plate 7.
[2] *The Art of India and Pakistan*, Plate 85.

of Indian music) *nayakas* and *nayikas* (the ideal lovers) and *barahmasas* (the twelve months) while in the case of Malwa, there was the added theme of Sanskrit love-poetry. Krishna the god was rarely celebrated and it was rather as 'the best of lovers' that he was sometimes introduced into pictures. In a Bundi series depicting the twelve months, courtly lovers are shown sitting in a balcony watching a series of rustic incidents proceeding below. The lover, however, is not an ordinary prince but Krishna himself, his blue skin and royal halo leaving no possible doubt as to his real identity.[1] Similarly in paintings illustrating the character and personality of musical modes, Krishna was often introduced as the perfect embodiment of passionate loving. None of the poems accompanying the modes make any allusion to him. Indeed, their prime purpose is to woo the presiding genius of the melody and suggest the visual scene most likely to evoke its spirit. The musical mode, *Bhairava Raga*, for example, was actually associated with Siva, yet because the character of the music suggested furious passion the central figure of the lover dallying with a lady was depicted as Krishna.[2] In *Hindola Raga*, a mode connected with swinging, a similar result ensued. Swinging in Indian sentiment was normally associated with the rains and these in turn evoked 'memory and desire.' The character of the music was therefore visualized as that of a young prince swinging in the rain—his very movements symbolizing the act of love. Since Krishna, however, was the perfect lover, nothing was easier than to portray *Hindola Raga* as Krishna himself. *Hindola* might be invoked in the poem, but it was Krishna who appeared seated on the swing.[3] An exactly similar process occurred in the case of *Megh Mallar Raga*. This was connected with the rainy season, yet because rain and storm were symbolic of sex, *Megh Mallar* was portrayed not as a separate figure, but as Krishna once again dancing in the rain with ladies accompanying him. Even feminine modes of music suffered the same kind of transformation. *Vasanta Ragini*, 'the music of springtime,' was normally apostrophized as a lovely lady, yet because springtime suggested lovers, she was shown in painting as if she were Krishna dancing with a vase of flowers, holding a wand in his hand or celebrating the spring fertility festival. The mode, *Pancham Ragini*, was also feminine in character and was conceived of as a beauty enjoying her lover's advances. The lady herself was portrayed, yet once again Krishna was introduced, this time as her lover. In all these cases the celebration of Krishna was incidental to the main theme and only in one instance—a Malwa *Rasika Priya*—

[1] Plate 32.   [2] Plate 34.   [3] Plate 33.

is there a trace of undisguised adoration. In this lovely series,[1] Krishna's enchantment is perfectly suggested by the flowering trees which wave above him, the style acquiring an even more intense lyricism on account of its divine subject.

During the eighteenth century, painting in Rajasthan became increasingly secular, even artists of Udaipur devoting themselves almost exclusively to scenes of court life. The Ranas and the Mewar nobility were depicted hunting in the local landscape, watching elephant fights or moving in procession. Similar fashions prevailed in Jodhpur, Jaisalmer, Bikaner, Bundi and Kotah. Only, in fact, in two Rajasthan States and then for only brief periods was there any major celebration of the Krishna theme. At Kishangarh, a small State midway between Ajmer and Jaipur, a series of intensely poetic paintings were produced between the years 1750 and 1760— the prime stimulus being the delight of Raja Sawant Singh in Krishna's romance.[2] Born in 1699, Sawant Singh had ascended the throne in 1748 and given all his time to three activities, the rapturous re-living of Krishna's romance with Radha, the composition of ecstatic poems and the daily worship of Krishna as lover god. So great was his devotion that in 1757 be abandoned the throne and taking with him his favourite maid of honour, the beautiful poetess, Bani Thani, retired to Brindaban where he died in 1764. Sawant Singh's delight seems to have been shared by a local artist, Nihal Chand, for under the Raja's direction he produced a number of pictures in which Radha and Krishna sustained the leading roles. The pictures were mainly illustrations of Sawant Singh's own poems —the lovers being portrayed at moments of blissful wonder, drifting on a lake in a scarlet boat, watching fireworks cascading down the sky or gently dallying in a marble pavilion.

> Here is Love's enchanted zone
> Here Time and the Firmament stand still
> Here the Bride and Bridegroom
> Never can grow old.
> Here the fountains never cease to play
> And the night is ever young.[3]

Nihal Chand's style was eminently fitted to express this mood of sensitive adoration. Originally trained in the later Mughal style, he was able to render appearances with exquisite delicacy but was

[1] Bharat Kala Bhawan, Banaras.
[2] Eric Dickinson, 'The Way of Pleasure: the Kishangarh Paintings', *Marg*, Vol. III, No. 4, 29–35.
[3] Ibid., 31.

also acutely aware of rhythmical elegance. And it is this which constantly characterized his work, his greatest achievement being the creation of a local manner for portraying Radha and Krishna.[1] Radha was endowed with great arched eyebrows and long eyes—the end of the eye being tilted so as to join the downward sweeping line of the eyebrow while Krishna was given a slender receding forehead and narrow waist. Each was made to seem the acme of elegance and the result was a conception of Krishna and his love as the very embodiment of aristocratic breeding.

The same sense of aristocratic loveliness is conveyed by a scene of dancing figures almost life size in the palace library at Jaipur.[2] Painted under Raja Pratap Singh (1779–1803) the picture shows ladies of the palace impersonating Radha and Krishna dancing together attended by girl musicians.[3] Against a pale green background, the figures, dressed in greenish yellow, pale greyish blue and the purest white, posture with calm assured grace, while the pure tones and exquisite line-work invest the scene with gay and luminous clarity. We do not know the circumstances in which this great picture was painted but the existence of another large-scale picture portraying the circular dance—the lines of cowgirls revolving like flowers, with Radha and Krishna swaying in their midst—suggests that the Krishna theme had once again inflamed a Rajput ruler's imagination.[4]

Such groups of paintings are, at most, exquisite exceptions and it is rather in the Rajput states of the Punjab Hills—an area remote and quite distinct from Rajasthan—that the theme of Krishna the divine lover received its most enraptured expression in the eighteenth century. Until the second half of the seventeenth century this stretch of country bordering the Western Himalayas seems to have had no kind of painting whatsoever. In 1678, however, Raja Kirpal Pal inherited the tiny state of Basohli and almost immediately a new artistic urge became apparent. Pictures were produced on a scale comparable to that of Udaipur thirty years earlier and at the same time a local style of great emotional intensity makes its sudden appearance.[5] This new Basohli style, with its flat planes of brilliant green, brown, red, blue and orange, its savage profiles and great

[1] Plate 39.
[2] For cartoons of this picture, see A. K. Coomaraswamy, *Indian Drawings* (London, 1912), Vol. II, Plate 2 and *Rajput Painting*, Vol. II, Plates 9 and 10.
[3] Note 22.
[4] Gangoly, *Masterpieces of Rajput Painting*, Plate 10.
[5] Plates 4, 10, 26, 27, 30 and 31. *The Art of India and Pakistan*, Plates 100–102.

intense eyes has obvious connections with Udaipur paintings of the 1650–60 period. And although exact historical proof is still wanting, the most likely explanation is that under Rana Raj Singh some Udaipur artists were persuaded to migrate to Basohli. We know that Rajput rulers in the Punjab Hills were often connected by marriage with Rajput families in Rajasthan and it is therefore possible that during a visit to Udaipur, Raja Kirpal Pal recruited his atelier. Udaipur painting, however, can hardly have been the only source for even in its earliest examples Basohli painting has a smooth polish, a savage sophistication and a command of shading which suggests the influence of the Mughal style of Delhi. We must assume, in fact, a series of influences determined to a great extent by Raja Kirpal Pal's political contacts, his private journeys and individual taste, but perhaps above all by an urge to express his feelings for Krishna in a novel and personal manner. The result is not only a new style but a special choice of subject-matter. The *Rasika Priya* and the *Bhagavata Purana*, the texts so greatly favoured at Udaipur, were discarded and in their place Basohli artists produced a series of isolated scenes from Krishna's life—the child Krishna stealing butter,[1] Krishna the gallant robbing the cowgirls or exacting toll, Krishna extinguishing the forest-fire,[2] Krishna the violent lover devouring Radha with hungry eyes. Their greatest achievements, however, were two versions of Bhanu Datta's *Rasamanjari*, one of them completed in 1695,[3] shortly after Raja Kirpal Pal's death, the other almost certainly fifteen years earlier.[4] The text in question is a treatise on poetics illustrating how romantic situations should best be treated in Sanskrit poetry—the conduct of mature mistresses, experienced lovers, sly go-betweens, clowns or jokers being all subjected to analysis.[5] The subject of the text is secular romantic poetry and Krishna himself is never mentioned. None the less, in producing their illustrations, the artists made Krishna the central figure and we can only conclude that eschewing the obvious *Rasika Priya*, Raja Kirpal Pal had directed his artists to do for Sanskrit what Keshav Das had done for Hindi poetry—to celebrate Krishna as the most varied and skilled of lovers and as a corollary show him in a whole variety of romantic and poetic situations. As a result Krishna was portrayed in a number of highly conflicting roles—as husband, rake, seducer, paramour and gallant.

[1] Plate 4.
[2] Plate 10.
[3] Archer, *Indian Painting in the Punjab Hills*, Fig. 6.
[4] Plate 30. Coomaraswamy, *Boston Catalogue, V, Rajput Painting*, Plates 92–95.
[5] Note 23.

In one picture he is 'a gallant whose word cannot be trusted' and we see him in the act of delicately disengaging a lady's dress and gazing at her with passion-haunted eyes. The poem on the reverse runs as follows:

> Showing her a beautiful girdle
> Drawing on a fair panel with red chalk
> Putting a bracelet on her wrists
> And laying a necklace on her breasts
> Winning the confidence of the fawn-eyed lady of fair brows
> He slyly loosens the knot of her skirt
> Below the girdle-stead, with naughty hand.[1]

In another picture, he appears as 'a gallant well versed in the ways of courtesans,' the dreaded seducer of inexperienced girls. He is now shown approaching a formal pavilion, set in a lonely field. Inside the pavilion is the lovely object of his attack, sitting with a companion, knowing that willy-nilly she must shortly yield yet timidly making show of maidenly reserve.

> His swollen heart
> Knows neither shame nor pity
> Nor any fear of anger
> How can such a tender bud as I
> Be cast into his hands today?[2]

In yet a third picture, he is portrayed standing outside a house while the lady, the subject of his passions, sits within. He is once again 'a false gallant,' his amorous intentions being shown by the orange, a conventional symbol for the breasts, poised lightly in his hand. As the lady turns to greet him, she puts a dot in the circle which she has just drawn on the wall—a gesture which once again contains a hint of sex. On the picture's reverse the poem records a *conversation galante*.

> 'Beloved, what are you doing
> With a golden orange in your hand?'
> So said the moon-faced one
> Placing a dot
> On the bright circles
> Painted in the house.[3]

In other pictures, a clown or jester appears, introducing a witty joking element into the scene and thus presenting Krishna's attitude to love as all-inclusive.

[1] Coomaraswamy, *Boston Catalogue, V, Rajput Painting*, 171.
[2] Ibid., 172.   [3] Ibid., 173.

THE KRISHNA OF PAINTING

From 1693, the year of Raja Kirpal's death, painting at Basohli concentrated mainly on portraying rulers and on illustrating *ragas* and *raginis*—the poems which interpreted the moods and spirit of music. The style maintained its fierce intensity but there was now a gradual rounding of faces and figures, leading to a slight softening of the former brusque vigour. Devotion to Krishna does not seem to have bulked quite so largely in the minds of later Basohli rulers, although the cult itself may well have continued to exert a strong emotional appeal. In 1730, a Basohli princess, the lady Manaku, commissioned a set of illustrations to the *Gita Govinda* and Krishna's power to enchant not only the male but also the female mind was once again demonstrated.[1]

This series of illustrations is in some ways a turning point in Indian painting for not only was it to serve as a model and inspiration to later artists but its production brings to a close the most creative phase in Basohli art. After 1730, painting continued to be practised there but no longer with the same fervour. Basohli artists seem to have carried the style to other states—to Guler, Jammu, Chamba, Kulu, Nurpur and Bilaspur—but it is not until 1770 that the Krishna theme again comes into prominence. In about this year, artists from Guler migrated to the distant Garhwal, a large and straggling state at the far south of the Punjab Hills, taking with them a style of exquisite naturalism which had gradually reached maturity under the Guler ruler, Raja Govardhan Singh.[2] During his reign, a family of Kashmiri Brahmans skilled in the Mughal technique had joined his court and had there absorbed a new romantic outlook. On at least three occasions they had illustrated scenes from the *Bhagavata Purana*—Nanda celebrating Krishna's birth,[3] Krishna rescuing Nanda from the python which had started to devour his foot,[4] and finally the game of blind man's buff[5]—but their chief subject had been the tender enchantments of courtly love. Ladies were portrayed longing for their lovers. The greatest emphasis was placed on elegance of pose. Fierce distortions were gradually discarded and the whole purpose of painting was to dwell on exquisite figures and to suggest a rapt devotion to the needs of love.

It is this suavely delicate art which now appears in Garhwal. Among the Guler painters was a master-artist and although his first Garhwal pictures are concerned with passionate romance, devotion

[1] Plates 26 and 27. *The Art of India and Pakistan*, Plate 102.
[2] Archer, *Garhwal Painting*, 1–4.   [3] Gangoly, op. cit., Plate 35.
[4] Archer, *Indian Painting in the Punjab Hills*, Fig. 23.
[5] Mehta, *Studies in Indian Painting*, Plate 21.

to Krishna quickly becomes apparent.[1] The great Alaknanda River which roared through Srinagar, the capital, had a special fascination for him and just as Leonardo da Vinci evinced at one time a passionate interest in springing curls, the Guler artist found a special excitement in winding eddies and dashing water. The result was a sudden new interpretation of the Krishna theme. In two pictures where Krishna is shown quelling the snake Kaliya,[2] all the Guler qualities of elegant naturalism are abundantly present. Each figure has a smooth suavity and in every face there appears a look of calm adoration. It is the swirling, curling water, however, which gives the pictures their special Garhwal quality. The play of water evokes a melody of line and the result is a sense of upsurging joy. A similar religious exaltation marks other pictures by this master. At some time he appears to have been commissioned to illustrate the tale of Sudama the poor Brahman whose tattered hovel is changed by Krishna into a golden palace. He was evidently assisted by a weaker painter but in the pictures which are clearly his own work, the same quality of lyrical incantation appears. As Sudama journeys to Dwarka Krishna's golden city, his heart swoons with adoration, the hills, trees and ocean appear to dance about him and once again, the linear music of the composition engenders a feeling of supreme ecstasy.[3] We do not know which member of the Garhwal court acted as his patron—it is even possible that it was not the ruler himself but his consort, the Guler princess whom he had married in about the year 1770. What, at any rate, is clear is that at least one lively adorer of Krishna existed at the Garhwal court and that until the Gurkha invasions of 1803, there were other painters, besides the master-artist, who were similarly encouraged to interpret the Krishna theme.[4] Their style was clearly influenced by that of the master but in their use of slender leafless branches and towering spikes of blossom, they developed a special Garhwal imagery designed to suggest the slender beauty of love-enchanted girls. After the expulsion of the Gurkhas in 1816, a new Raja revived Garhwal painting. Krishna the lover was once again portrayed and until the middle of the nineteenth century, pictures continued to be produced blending the delights of courtly passion with adoration of God.

It was in the state of Kangra, however, that the greatest developments occurred. In 1775, the young Sansar Chand became Raja, and despite his extreme youth, quickly acquired mastery of the Kangra court. It is unlikely that artists were immediately sum-

[1] Plates 19, 20 and 35.   [2] Coomaraswamy, *Rajput Painting*, Plates 53 and 54.
[3] Archer, *Garhwal Painting*, Plate 1.   [4] Plates 7, 12 and 25.

moned, but certainly by 1780 a flourishing school of painters had come into existence.[1] As at Garhwal, the artists of Kangra came originally from Guler and thus a similar phenomenon arises—the Guler manner providing the basis for yet a second great style. Sansar Chand was obviously quite exceptional, for not only was he successful in politics and war, but from his early manhood was devoted to Krishna as lover god. And it is this all-absorbing interest which explains the vast expansion of painting which now occurred. Under Sansar Chand's stimulus artists began to portray every situation involving Krishna, the cowherd. He was shown as a baby crying for the moon, being washed by his foster-mother, Yasoda, or mischievously breaking pitchers full of curds. He would be painted strolling with the cowherds, playing on his flute, or bringing the cattle home at evening. But the main theme to which the artists constantly returned was his main cowgirl love. Radha would be shown standing with Krishna in the forest, gazing trustfully into his eyes, seeking shelter with him from the rain or sitting with him by a stream.[2] Sometimes she and the cowgirls were shown celebrating the spring festival of Holi, Krishna syringing them with tinted water while they themselves strove to return his onslaughts by throwing red powder.[3] Often the scene would shift from the forest to the village, and Krishna would then be shown gazing at Radha as she dried herself after bathing or squatted in a courtyard cooking food. At other times he appeared assisting her at her toilet, helping her to dress her hair or applying a beauty mark to her forehead. If the scene was night itself, Radha would be shown sitting in her chamber, while far away across the courtyards and gardens would loom the small figure of Krishna waiting lonely on a bed. Occasionally the lovers would be portrayed expressing their rapture by means of simple gestures. Krishna's arm would be shown placed lovingly around Radha's shoulders, or Radha herself would be portrayed hiding her head on Krishna's breast.[4] In all these pictures, the style had an innocent and exquisite clarity, suggesting by its simple unaffected naturalism the artists' delight in Krishna's character, their appreciation of the feminine mind, their sense of sex as inherently noble and their association of romance with God himself.

It is in a series of illustrations to certain texts, however, that Kangra painting reaches its greatest heights. Among the many artists employed by Sansar Chand, a certain Purkhu was notable for

[1] Archer, *Kangra Painting*, 2-5. [2] Ibid., Plate 2.
[3] Ibid., Plate 1. [4] Ibid., Plate 2.

his 'remarkable clearness of tone and delicacy of handling,'[1] and though none of his pictures are signed it is these qualities which characterize one of the two most famous sets of illustrations executed in Kangra. The subject was the tenth book of the *Bhagavata Purana* and the scenes illustrated ranged from Krishna's birth and adventures with demons to his frolics with the cowgirls and final slaughter of Kansa. Purkhu's style—if Purkhu is indeed the master responsible —is remarkable for its luminous clarity, its faint suggestions of modelling, and above all for its natural use of rhythm. In every scene,[2] cowherds appear engaged in different tasks, yet throughout there is a sense of oneness with Krishna himself. Krishna is shown delighting all by his simple friendliness and dignified charm and the style itself endows each scene with gentle harmony.

Purkhu was clearly one of the greatest artists ever to practise in the Punjab Hills, but it is a certain Kushala who is supposed to have been Sansar Chand's special favourite. We do not know which pictures are by his hand but there exist two series of illustrations of such distinctive quality that Kushala may well have been responsible.[3] One is a series of paintings illustrating part of Bihari's *Sat Sai*—the seven-hundred poems in which he extolled Krishna's love-making.[4] The other is yet another version of the *Gita Govinda* where Krishna is shown consorting with the cowgirls in blissful abandon.[5] In both these series, the inherent loveliness of Radha and the cowgirls is expressed by supple flowing line, a flair for natural posture and the inclusion of poetic images. The scarlet of a cowgirl's skirt is echoed by the redness of a gathering storm, the insertion of Krishna into the background suggesting the passionate nature of their imminent embraces.[6] In a similar way, the forest itself is 'threaded with phases of passion' and slender trees in flower parallel the slim romantic girls who long for Krishna's love.

One other Kangra master remains to be mentioned. Besides the pictures already noted, there exists a further series illustrating the tenth book of the *Bhagavata Purana*. The artist's identity is once again uncertain, but just as the Garhwal master was fascinated by the swirl of curling water, the Kangra artist in question delighted in

[1] B. H. Baden Powell, *Handbook of the Manufactures and Arts of the Punjab* (Lahore, 1872), 355. Purkhu must now, most probably, be connected with the first of the two Kangra masters described in *Kangra Painting* (p. 4)—Plates 3 and 4 being examples of his work. [2] Plates 3, 5, 6, 8, 9, 11 and 16.

[3] Archer, *Kangra Painting*, Plates 1 and 2; also p. 4 where the second of the two Kangra masters is described.

[4] Plate 36; Mehta, op. cit., Plates 25 and 26.   [5] Plate 21.

[6] Mehta, op. cit., Plate 22.

the blonde pallor of the Indian moon.[1] Each incident in the text is rendered as if in moonlight—a full moon riding in the sky, its pale reflection shining in water, the countryside itself bathed throughout in frosty whiteness. As a result the figures of Radha and the cowgirls seem imbued with pallid glamour, their love for Krishna with an almost unearthly radiance.

Kangra painting continued throughout the nineteenth century but it was only during Sansar Chand's own reign (1775-1823) that the style achieved great lyrical glory. Similarly it was only towards the end of the eighteenth century that other states in the Punjab Hills developed their own interpretations of the great impassioned theme. At Nurpur, Chamba, Kulu and Bilaspur[2] pictures of Krishna had temporary vogues and at all these places artists created new modes of expression. None of the local styles, however, possessed the same prestige as that of Kangra and all were subsequently obliterated by the general Kangra manner. By the mid-nineteenth century, the Rajput order in the Punjab Hills foundered before the British and while lesser nobles and merchants continued to purchase pictures of Krishna the cult as a whole declined in princely favour. Only in Eastern India and then mainly in the villages did delight in Krishna continue to evoke new painting. From the twelfth century onwards Bengal had constantly celebrated the loves of Krishna—the poets Jayadeva, Chandi Das and Vidyapati being all natives of this part of India. Hymns to Krishna were sung in the villages and as part of this fervid adhesion, local manuscripts of the *Bhagavata Purana* and the *Gita Govinda* were often produced. Such manuscripts were normally not illustrated but were preserved between wooden covers, on which scenes of Krishna dancing with the cowgirls or with male devotees were painted.[3] Book covers of this kind were produced in the seventeenth and eighteenth centuries and the resulting pictures have something of the savage elation associated with the Basohli style and its derivatives. During the nineteenth century, painted book-covers ceased to be produced but three other kinds of painting continued to celebrate the Krishna theme. Frescoes of Hindu gods and goddesses including Krishna were often executed on the mud walls of village houses in Mithila, the birthplace of the poet Vidyapati, and the style of painting with its brilliant colours and brusque distortions testified to the great excitement still engendered by Krishna's name.[4] At Kalighat near Calcutta, a special

[1] Plates 13-15.　　　　　　　　　　　　　　　　[2] Plate 18.
[3] *The Art of India and Pakistan*, Plate 79.
[4] W. G. Archer, 'Maithil Painting,' *Marg*, Vol. III, No. 2.

type of water-colour picture was mass-produced for sale to pilgrims and although the stock subjects included almost every Hindu god, many incidents from Krishna's life were boldly portrayed.[1] The style with its curving sumptuous forms is more a clue to general Bengali interests than to any special attitudes to Krishna, but the pictures, strangely parallel in style to the work of the modern artist Fernand Léger, have a robust gaiety and bounding vigour, not inappropriate to the Krishna theme. The third type of painting is the work of professional village minstrels known as *jadupatuas*. As a means of livelihood, *jadupatuas* travel from village to village in West Bengal, entertaining the people by singing ballads and illustrating their songs with long painted scrolls. As each ballad proceeds, the scroll is slowly unwound, one scene leading to another until the whole is concluded. Among the ballads thus intoned, the romance of Krishna is among the most common and the style of painting with its crude exuberance suggests the strength of popular devotion.[2]

There remains one last form of painting. During the twentieth century, the modern movement in Indian art has produced at least four major artists—Rabindranath Tagore, Amrita Sher-Gil, Jamini Roy and George Keyt. Of these four, the first two did not illustrate the Krishna theme. Jamini Roy, on the other hand, has often painted Krishna as flute-player and dancer.[3] It would be unrealistic to suggest that these pictures spring from a lively sense of Krishna as God—Jamini Roy has, in fact, resorted to themes of Christ with equal, if not greater, frequency but has shown no signs of becoming a Christian. It is rather that in painting these pictures, he has treated Krishna as a symbol of rural vitality, a figure whose boisterous career among the cowherds is an exact reflection of his own attitudes and enthusiasms. To Jamini Roy, the Bengali village with its sense of rude health is infinitely to be preferred to a city such as Calcutta with its artificiality and disease and in a style of bold simplifications, he has constantly celebrated the natural vigour and inherent dignity of simple unsophisticated men.

Such pictures stress a comparatively unimportant side of Krishna's character and it is rather in the paintings of George Keyt that Krishna the lover is proudly portrayed. Born in Ceylon of mixed ancestry, Keyt has, for many years, been acutely responsive to

[1] W. G. Archer, *Bazaar Paintings of Calcutta* (London, 1953), Plates 8, 9, 14, 19, 30, 31 and 41.

[2] Ajit Mookerjee, *Art of India*, (Calcutta, 1952) Fig. 94.

[3] B. Dey and J. Irwin, 'Jamini Roy,' *Journal of the Indian Society of Oriental Art* (1944), Vol. XII, Plate 6.

Indian poetry. In 1947, he published the translation of the *Gita Govinda*, excerpts from which have been quoted in the text, and throughout his career his work has been distinguished by a poet's delight in feminine form and sensuous rapture. To Keyt such a delight is a vital component of adult minds and in the romance of Radha and Krishna he found a subject subtly expressive of his own most intimate beliefs. His paintings and line-drawings of Radha, Krishna and the cowgirls—at once modern yet vitally Indian in spirit—have the same qualities as those in the *Gita Govinda*.[1] Radha and Krishna are shown luxuriating in each other's elegance, a certain ineffable tenderness characterizing their gestures and movements. Their love is gentle rather than brusque, an air of glamorous wonder broods above them and we meet once more that blend of romantic sensuality and loving innocence which is perhaps the chief Indian contribution to cultured living. It is this quality which gives to Indian paintings of Krishna and his loves their incomparable fervour, and makes them enduring expressions of Indian religion.

[1] For reproductions of Keyt's work, see Martin Russell, *George Keyt* (Bombay, 1950), Plates 1–101.

NOTES

Note 1, p. 13.
For a further discussion of these two main kinds of Indian expression, see my *Indian Painting* (Iris, Batsford, London, 1956).

Note 2, p. 14.
In Indian painting, Krishna is normally blue or mauve in colour, though cases occur in which he is black, green or dark brown. Black would seem to follow from Krishna's name—the word 'Krishna' meaning 'black'—and may have been applied either because he sprang from a black hair of Vishnu or because he was born at midnight, 'black as a thundercloud.' It has been suggested that his dark complexion proves a Dravidian or even an aboriginal origin since both the Dravidian races and the aboriginal tribes are dark brown in colour in contrast to the paler Aryans. None of the texts, however, appears to corroborate this theory. So far as 'blue' and 'mauve' are concerned, 'blue' is the colour of Vishnu and characterizes most of his incarnations. As the colour of the sky, it is appropriate to a deity who was originally associated with the sun—the sun with its life-giving rays according well with Vishnu's role as loving protector. 'Blue' is also supposed to be the colour of the ocean on which Vishnu is said to recline at the commencement of each age. In view of the variations in colour in the pictures, it is perhaps significant that 'blue,' 'mauve' and 'green' are commonly regarded in village India as variants of 'black'—many Indians making no distinction between them. In Indian painting, the fact that Krishna is blue makes it easy to identify him, his only serious rival being another and earlier incarnation of Vishnu, the princely Rama. The latter can usually be distinguished from Krishna by the fact that he carries a bow (never a cowherd's stick) and is often accompanied by Hanuman, the monkey leader.

Note 3, p. 17.
For a comparison of Ghora Angirasa's teaching in the *Chandogya Upanishad* with Krishna's precepts in the *Gita*, see Mazumdar, *The Age of Imperial Unity* (432-4) and Basham, *The Wonder that was India* (242-7, 304-5).

Note 4, p. 17.
Although the actual date of the *Mahabharata* war has been variously assessed—'between 1400 and 1000 B.C.' (M. A. Mehendale in *The Age of Imperial Unity*, 251) 'the beginning of the ninth century B.C. (Basham, op. cit., 39)—the epic itself is generally recognized as being a product of many centuries of compilation. The portions relating to Krishna the hero may well date from the third century B.C. The *Gita*, on the other hand, was possibly composed in the second century B.C. 'but assumed

the form in which it appears in the *Mahabharata* today in the early centuries A.D.' (Mehendale, op. cit., 249).

Note 5, p. 24.

The implication is that the Pandavas have not been granted ultimate salvation i.e. final release from living but have reached the important transitional level of 'the heaven of the doers of good deeds.' They have also been granted the limited status of petty gods.

Note 6, p. 25.

Harivansa, 'the Genealogy of Krishna' but more literally, 'the Genealogy of Hari,' a synonym for Vishnu. For the sake of clearness and to avoid burdening the text with too much periphrasis, I have throughout referred to Krishna as such. In the texts themselves, however, he is constantly invoked under other names—Hari (or Vishnu), Govinda (the cowherd), Keshava (the hairy or radiant one), Janarddana (the most worshipful), Damodara ('bound with a rope,' referring to the incident (p. 32) when having been tied by Yasoda to a mortar, Krishna uproots the two trees), Murari ('foe of Mura, the arch demon' p. 58) or in phrases such as 'queller of Kaliya the snake,' 'destroyer of Kesi, the demon horse,' 'slayer of Madhu—the demon who sprang from the ear of Vishnu and was killed by him.' A similar use of periphrasis occurs in Anglo-Saxon kennings ('world-candle' for sun, 'battle-adders' for arrows). In the same way, Abul Fazl's chronicle, the *Akbarnama*, never names the emperor Akbar but refers to him in terms such as 'His Majesty,' 'the holy soul,' 'lord of the age,' 'fountain of generosity,' 'the sacred heart,' 'the world-adorning mind,' 'the decorated mansion of sports.'

Note 7, p. 26, 34, 46, 68, 69.

In Chapters 3 and 4 I have, in the main, strictly followed the *Bhagavata Purana*, incorporating, however, a few important details and passages either not given in this text but included in the *Vishnu Purana* or if given, not so vividly expressed. The details and passages in question are page 27 concerning the white and black hairs of Vishnu, page 34—the lyrical description of Krishna's life in the forest, page 46—Akrura's meditation as he goes to visit Krishna, page 68—the drunken brawl and page 69 the deaths of Balarama and Krishna. All extracts are from H. H. Wilson, *The Vishnu Purana* (pages 498, 511, 541–2, 609–612).

Note 8, p. 28.

The resemblance between Kansa's order to kill all male infants and Herod's slaughter of the innocents has often been remarked.

Note 9, p. 29.

Krishna's constant alterations of role, appearing sometimes as God but more often as boy or man, have been commented on by Isherwood and Prabhavananda in connection with Arjuna's dilemma in the *Mahabharata*. 'Krishna is the divine incarnation of Vishnu, Arjuna's chosen deity. Arjuna knows this—yet, by a merciful ignorance, he sometimes forgets. Indeed, it is Krishna who makes him forget, since no ordinary man could bear the strain of constant companionship with God. After the vision of Krishna's divine aspect, Arjuna is appalled by the realization that he has been treating the Lord of the universe as 'friend and fellow-mortal.' He humbly begs Krishna's pardon, but his awe soon leaves him. Again, he has forgotten. We may infer the same relationship between Jesus and his disciples after the vision of the transfiguration.' (*The Song of God, Bhagavad-Gita*, 29–30).

Note 10, p. 33.

Although part of the supreme Trinity, Brahma was often treated in literature as an ordinary god who ambled gently about the world, was often rather absent-minded, sometimes behaved as if he were a priest, and was prone, as on the present occasion, to act a trifle misguidedly.

Note 11, p. 40.

The scene is illustrated in two Kangra and Guler paintings (Archer, *Indian Painting in the Punjab Hills*, Figs. 10 and 23.

Note 12, p. 58.

Pragjyotisha—a city situated in the east, in Kamarupa on the borders of Assam. According to the *Vishnu Purana* (Wilson, 582), its environs were defended by 'nooses, constructed by the demon Mura (Naraka's ally), the edges of which were as sharp as razors.' Mura had seven thousand sons (not seven, as stated in the *Bhagavata*). All, however, were 'burnt like moths with the flame of the edge of Krishna's discus.'

Note 13, p. 67.

Basham (op. cit., 305) points out that elements in the Krishna story such as the destruction of the Yadavas and the death of the god are 'quite un-Indian in their tragic character. The themes of the drunken brawl leading to a general slaughter, of the hero slain by an arrow piercing his one vulnerable spot, and of the great city engulfed by the sea, are well-known in European epic literature, but do not occur elsewhere in that of India and are not hinted at in the Vedas. The concept of the dying god, so widespread in the ancient Near East, is found nowhere else in Indian mythology.'

It is unfortunate that Krishna's reasons for destroying the Yadava race are nowhere made very clear. The affront to the Brahmans is the immediate occasion for the slaughter but hardly its actual cause; and, if it is argued that the Yadavas must first be destroyed in order to render Krishna's withdrawal from the world complete, we must then assume that the Yadavas are in some mysterious way essential parts of Krishna himself. Such a status, however, does not seem to be claimed for them and none of the texts suggest that this is so. The slaughter, therefore, remains an enigma.

Note 14, p. 68.

Wilson (op. cit., 608) summarizing the portents listed in the *Mahabharata* but not included in the *Vishnu* or *Bhagavata Puranas*.

Note 15, p. 72.

From the *Brihadaranyaka*, quoted A. Danielou, 'An Approach to Hindu Erotic Sculpture,' *Marg*, Vol. II, No. 1, 88. For a Western expression of this point of view, compare Eric Gill, 'Art and Love,' *Rupam* (Calcutta, 1925), No. 21, 5.

'If the trees and rocks, the thunder and the sea, the frightful avidity of animal life and the loveliness of flowers are so many hints of the God who made them, how much more obviously are the things of humanity analogues of the things of God? And among all such things, the union of man and woman takes the highest place and is the most potent symbol. Therefore it is that outside the commercial civilizations of the western world, love and marriage take their place as types of divine union and everywhere love and marriage are the subject matter, the theme of religious writers, singers, painters and sculptors. It is true that love is the theme of western writers also but with them the idea of love is entirely free from divine signification. (As a corollary), the more the divine background disappears, the more the prudishness of the police becomes the standard of ethics and aesthetics alike. Under such an aegis the arts are necessarily degraded to the level of the merely sentimental or the merely sensual and while the sentimental is everywhere applauded, the sensual is a source of panic.'

Note 16, p. 73.

In later poetry as well as in popular worship, Radha's position is always that of an adored mistress—never that of a beloved wife. And it is outside or rather in the teeth of marriage that her romance with Krishna is prosecuted. Such a position clearly involved a sharp conflict with conventional morals and in the fourteenth century, an attempt was made, in the *Brahma Vaivarta Purana*, to re-write the *Bhagavata Purana*, magnifying Radha as leader of the cow-girls, disguising or rather denying her adultery and finally presenting her as Krishna's eternal consort. For this purpose, three hypotheses were adopted. Radha was throughout assumed to be Krishna's spouse and it is only on account of a curse that she takes human form as a cowgirl and comes to live in Brindaban. Radha herself does not marry Ayana the cowherd—his wedding being only with her shadow. Thirdly, Krishna comes to Brindaban and goes through a secret marriage with her. Their love-making is, therefore, no longer adulterous but strictly conjugal. It is not perhaps surprising that the *Brahma Vaivarta Purana* failed to capture the Indian imagination and indeed is nowadays hardly ever heard of. It is of interest mainly on account of the prolific information given about Radha, the fact that it sets her firmly in the centre, dethroning the hapless Rukmini, and its baroque descriptions of sexual union.

Note 17, p. 73.

During the eleventh and twelfth centuries, a parallel situation seems to have arisen in feudal France and Germany where local love-poetry also treated adultery as a *sine qua non* of romance.

'Two things prevented the men of that age from connecting their ideal of romantic and passionate love with marriage. The first is, of course, the actual practice of feudal society. Marriages had nothing to do with

NOTES

love and no 'nonsense' about marriage was tolerated. All marriages were matches of interest and, worse still, of an interest that was continually changing. When the alliance which had answered would answer no longer, the husband's object was to get rid of the lady as quickly as possible. Marriages were frequently dissolved. The same woman who was the lady and 'the dearest dread' of her vassals was often little better than a piece of property to her husband. He was master in his own house. So far from being a natural channel for the new kind of love, marriage was rather the drab background against which that love stood out in all the contrast of its new tenderness and delicacy. The situation is indeed a very simple one, and not peculiar to the Middle Ages. Any idealization of sexual love, in a society where marriage is purely utilitarian, must begin by being an idealization of adultery.' (C. S. Lewis, *The Allegory of Love* (London, 1936), 13.)

Note 18, p. 77.

Much of the *Gita Govinda*'s power arises from the endowment of Nature with romantic ardour, the forest itself being presented as a highly sensitive and symbolic setting for the behaviour of lovers. The following passage from *Tess of the D'Urbervilles* is perhaps the nearest approach in English to this kind of treatment.

'Amid the oozing fatness and warm ferments of the Var Vale, at a season when the rush of juices could almost be heard below the hiss of fertilization, it was impossible that the most fanciful love should not grow passionate. The ready bosoms existing there were impregnated by their surroundings. July passed over their heads and the weather which came in its wake seemed an effort on the part of Nature to match the state of hearts at Talbothays Dairy. The air of the place, so fresh in the spring and early summer, was stagnant and enervating now. Its heavy scents weighed upon them, and at mid-day the landscape seemed lying in a swoon. Ethiopic scorchings browned the upper slopes of the pastures, but there was still bright herbage here where the water courses purled. And as Clare was oppressed by the outward heats, so was he burdened inwardly by waxing fervour of passion for the soft and silent Tess.'

Note 19, p. 77.

The *Gita Govinda* was one of the first Sanskrit poems to be rendered into English—Sir William Jones publishing a mellifluous version in *Asiatick Researches* in 1792. Later in the nineteenth century it was translated into Victorian verse by Sir Edwin Arnold. The present translation from which all the extracts are taken is by George Keyt, the foremost modern artist of Ceylon. It is greatly to be hoped that the entire translation, hitherto available only in an Indian edition, will one day be published in England.

Note 20, p. 86.

Poems 1 and 2 are based on versions by O. C. Gangoly (*Masterpieces of Rajput Painting*, 29, 58); poems 3–11 are from new translations by Deben Bhattacharya.

Note 21, p. 91.

For the originals of certain poems in the *Rasika Priya* and their literal translation, see Coomaraswamy, 'The Eight Nayikas.'

Note 22, p. 104.

The first scholar to draw attention to this fact, i.e. that the subjects are not Radha and Krishna but palace ladies impersonating them, is Dr. Joan van Lohuizen de Leeuw, whose paper on this and kindred problems is under preparation.

Note 23, p. 105.

For a detailed discussion of Bhanu Datta's *Rasamanjari* and of similar treatises by other Sanskrit authors, see V. Raghavan, *Srngaramanjari of Saint Akbar Shah* (Hyderabad, 1951).

BIBLIOGRAPHY

AGRAWALA, V. S.: 'The Romance of Himachal Paintings,' *Roopa-Lekha* XX, 2, (1948-9), 87-93.
ARCHER, W. G.: *Indian Painting in the Punjab Hills* (London, 1952). *Kangra Painting* (London, 1952). *Garhwal Painting* (London, 1954). *Indian Painting* (London, 1956).
BASHAM, A. L.: *The Wonder that was India* (London, 1954).
BURNOUF, E. (trans.): *Le Bhagavata Purana* (Paris, 1840-98).
COOMARASWAMY, A. C.: 'The Eight Nayikas,' *Journal of Indian Art and Industry*, XVI (New Series), No. 128 (1914), 99-116. *Rajput Painting* (Oxford, 1916). *Catalogue of the Indian Collections in the Museum of Fine Arts, Boston: Part V, Rajput Painting; Part VI, Mughal Painting* (Cambridge, Mass. 1926, 1930). (trans.) *The Taking of Toll* (London, 1915).
GANGOLY, O. C.: *Masterpieces of Rajput Painting* (Calcutta, 1926). *Ragas and Raginis* (Calcutta, 1934).
GRAY, B.: *Rajput Painting* (London, 1948). 'Painting,' *The Art of India and Pakistan*, ed. L. Ashton (London, 1950).
GRIERSON, G. A.: *The Modern Vernacular Literature of Hindustan* (Calcutta, 1889).
HENDLEY, T. H.: *Memorials of the Jeypore Exhibition. IV, the Razm Namah* (London, 1883).
HOLLINGS, W. (trans.): *The Prem Sagur* (Lucknow, 1880).
ISHERWOOD, C. and PRABHAVANANDA, S. (trans.): *The Song of God, Bhagavad-Gita* (London, 1947).
JONES, W. (trans.): 'Gitagovinda or Songs of Jayadeva,' *Asiatick Researches* (Calcutta, 1792).
KEYT, G. (trans.): *Sri Jayadeva's Gita Govinda* (Bombay, 1947).
MATHERS, E. POWYS (trans.): *Eastern Love* (London, 1927-30). (trans.) *Love Songs of Asia* (London, 1944).
MAZUMDAR, R. C.: (ed.) *The History and Culture of the Indian People, I, The Vedic Age* (London, 1951); *II, The Age of Imperial Unity* (Bombay, 1951).
MEHTA, N. C.: *Studies in Indian Painting* (Bombay, 1926). *Gujarati Painting in the Fifteenth Century* (London, 1931).
RANDHAWA, M. S.: *Kangra Valley Painting* (New Delhi, 1954). *The Krishna Legend in Pahari Painting* (New Delhi, 1956).
ROY, P. C. (trans.): *The Mahabharata* (Calcutta, 1883).
SEN, D. C.: *History of Bengali Language and Literature* (Calcutta, 1911).
SEN, R. N. (trans.): *The Brahma Vaivarta Purana* (Allahabad, 1920).
STCHOUKINE, I.: *La Peinture Indienne* (Paris, 1929).
WINTERNITZ, M.: *A History of Indian Literature* (Calcutta, I, 1927; II, 1933).
WILSON, H. H. (trans.): *The Vishnu Purana* (London, 1840).

INDEX

Abul Fazl, 116, pl. 1 (comment)
Aditi, mother of the gods, 58, 59
Age of Imperial Unity, The, 115, 121
Agni, god of fire, 18
Agrawala, V. S., 121
Ahmadnagar, Deccan, 97
Ajmer, Rajasthan, 103
Akbar, Mughal Emperor, 97–9, 116, pl. 1 (comment)
Akbarnama, 98, 116
Akrura, chief of the Yadavas, 45–7, 49, 51, 57, 116
Allegory of Love, The, 119
Altdorfer, 93
Amaru, Sanskrit poet, 73
Aniruddha, son of Pradyumna and grandson of Krishna, 64
Archer, Mildred, 4, 9
Archer, W. G., 4, 101, 105, 107–112, 115, 117, 121
Arjuna, leading Pandava, husband of Draupadi, husband of Krishna's sister, Subhadra, 20–2, 64, 65, 67, 69, 116, 117
Arnold, Sir Edwin, 119
Art of India and Pakistan, The, 96, 98, 101, 104, 107, 111, 121
Asiatick Researches, 119
Assam, 117
Aurangzeb, Mughal Emperor, 99
Ayana, husband of Radha, brother of Yasoda, 72, 118

Baden Powell, B. H., 110
Bakasura, crane demon, 33
Balagopala Stuti, poem by Bilvamangala, 84, 94
Balarama, brother of Krishna, 27, 30, 31, 34–6, 44–8, 50–6, 61–4, 66, 67, 69, 116, pls. 1, 5, 6, 9, 12, 16, 17
Bali, ruler of the underworld, 62
Bani Thani, poetess of Kishangarh, 103
Barahmasa, poems of the twelve months, 102, pl. 32
Basawan, Mughal artist, pls. 1, 2 (comment), 3 (comment)
Basham, A. L., 9, 19, 115, 117, 121
Basohli, Punjab Hills, 104, 105, 107, 111, pls. 18 (comment), 26 (comment), 30 (comment)
Beatty, Sir Chester, pls. 17, 19
Bhagavad Gita, 15–17, 24, 67, 115, 117
Bhagavata Purana, 11, 25–71, 72, 74, 85, 95, 99, 101, 105, 107, 110, 111, 116–18, 121, pls. 3–19

Bhakti, devotion to God, 19, 24
Bhanu Datta, author of *Rasamanjari*, 9, 105, 120, pls. 30, 31
Bharat Kala Bhawan, Banaras, 103, pl. 37
Bharatiya Natya Sastra, Sanskrit treatise, 90
Bhartrihari, Sanskrit poet, 73
Bhattacharya, Deben, 9, 87–90, 119
Bhima, strongest of the five Pandavas, 24, 65, 66
Bihari Lal, poet, 84, 110, pl. 36
Bijapur, Deccan, 97
Bikaner, Rajasthan, 99, 100, 103
Bilaspur, Punjab Hills, 107, 111, pl. 18
Bilvamangala, poet, 84, 94
Blue, colour of Krishna, 14, 115
Book covers, Bengali, 111
Brahma, 17, 27, 28, 33, 34, 58, 59, 65, 67, 117, pl. 2
Brahma Vaivarta Purana, 118, 121
Brahmans, 22, 28, 30, 38, 39, 62, 63, 67, 68, 71, 74, 107, 108, 117
Wives of, 38, 39
Braj, country around Mathura, 26, 28, 40
Brihadaranyaka, 117
Brindaban, forest near Gokula, 33, 35, 45, 46, 49, 52, 53, 59–62, 103, pl. 6
British Museum, pl. 18
Brough, J., 9
Buddhism, 94
Bull demon, 44
Bundelkhand, 91, 99
Bundi, Rajasthan, 101–3
Burnouf, E., 121

Calcutta, 111, 112
Campbell, Roy, 75
Ceylon, 57, 112
Chamba, Punjab Hills, 107, 111
Chandi Das, Bengali poet, 84, 85, 89, 111
Chandigarh Art Gallery, East Punjab, pl. 27
Chandogya Upanishad, 17, 24, 115
Chanura, wrestler, 45, 48
Chawand, Mewar, 100
Christ, 14, 112, 117
Clothes, stealing of cowgirls', 37, 38, 74, 75, pl. 11
Coomaraswamy, A. K., 99, 104–6, 108, 120, 121, pl. 8 (comment)
Cowgirls, loves of the, 29, 36–8, 41–4, 46, 49, 50, 52, 53, 58, 60–2, 66, 70–82, 85, 86, 109, 110, 113, pls. 11, 13–15, 20–3.

123

THE LOVES OF KRISHNA

Cowherds, abandonment of, by Krishna, 49-53, 61, 62
  Krishna's life with, 30, 33-6, 38-40, 43-8, 70, 74, 85, 86, 112, pls. 5-7, 10, 12, 16, 17, 20

Damodara, pseudonym for Krishna, 116
Dance, circular, 38, 41, 43, 46, 74, 75, pl. 13 (comment)
Danielou, A., 117
Daruka, charioteer to Krishna, 68, 69
Demons, combats with, 29, 30, 33-6, 44, 45, 48, 54, 55, 58, 64, 116, 117, pl. 9
  role of, 18, 19
Devaka, younger brother of King Ugrasena, 27
Devaki, mother of Krishna, 17, 27, 28, 44, 46, 48-50, 52, 62, 69, pl. 3
Devi, goddess, Earth Mother, 28, 40, 56, pls. 3, 18
Dey, B., 112
Dharma, 18, 23
Dhenuka, ass demon, 34
Dhritarashtra, blind son of Kuru, father of Kauravas, 20, 21, 51, 66
Dice, contest by, 21
Dickinson, Eric, 103
Draupadi, daughter of King of Panchal, common wife of the five Pandavas, 20-3, 64, 67
Drumalika, demon, 26
Duryodhana, leading Kaurava and son of Dhritarashtra, 23, 51, 66, 67
Dwarka, Krishna's capital in Western India, 21, 22, 54-9, 61-4, 66-70, 94, 108, pls. 2 (comment), 19

Earth, 27, 49, 58, 67
Eastern Love, 121
El Greco, 93

Flute playing, 15, 36, 37, 41, 61, 78, 86, 109, 112, pl. 21
Forest fires, 35, 36, pl. 10
France, feudal, 118

Games with cowherds, Krishna's, 31-5, 45, pls. 4, 9
Gandhi, Mahatma, 15
Gangoly, O. C., 104, 119, 121
Garga, sage, 30, 31
Garhwal, Punjab Hills, 107-10, pl. 38 (comment)
Garhwal Painting, 107, 108, 121
Germany, feudal, 118
Ghora Angirasa, 17, 115
Gill, Eric, 118
Gita Govinda, Sanskrit poem by Jayadeva, 9, 11, 76-84, 94-6, 98, 107, 110, 111, 113, 119, 121, pls. 20-7
Gods, role of, 18, 19
Goetz, H., 99, 100

Gokula, district near Mathura, 26-30, 33, 44
Govardhan Singh, Raja of Guler, 107
Govardhana, greatest of the hills, 39, 40, 42, 59, pl. 12
Govind Das, poet, 84, 88
Govinda, pseudonym for Krishna, 116
Gray, Basil, 100, 121
Grierson, Sir G. A., 121
Grunewald, 93
Gujarati Painting in the Fifteenth Century, 121
Guler, Punjab Hills, 107-9, pl. 18 (comment)

Hari, pseudonym for Krishna, 116
Harivansa, appendix to *Mahabharata* epic, 25, 32, 98, 116
Hendley, T. H., 98, 121
Herod, 116
Holi festival, 109
Hollings, W., 121
Hunter, slayer of Krishna, see Jara.
Hussain Shah, ruler of Jaunpur, 96

India Office Library, London, pl. 34 (comment)
Indian Museum, Calcutta, pl. 35
Indian Painting, 115, 121
Indian Painting in the Punjab Hills, 105, 107
Indra, king of the gods, lord of the clouds, 18, 24, 39, 40, 46, 58, 59, 65, 66, pls. 2, 12
Irwin, J., 112
Isherwood, Christopher, 15, 24, 116, 121

Jadupatuas, minstrel artists of Bengal, 112
Jaipur, Rajasthan, 95, 98, 103, 104, pls. 1 (comment), 2 (comment)
Jaisalmer, Rajasthan, 103
Jambhavati, a queen of Krishna, 56, 57, 60
Jammu, Punjab Hills, 107
Janarddana, pseudonym for Krishna, 116
Japan, 13
Jara, Bhil hunter, slayer of Krishna, 24, 67, 69, pl. 2
Jarasandha, demon king of Magadha, 26, 54-6, 65
Jaunpur, Eastern India, 96, 97
Jayadeva, Sanskrit poet, 76, 77, 84, 94, 111, 121
Jodhpur, Rajasthan, 95, 103
Jones, Sir William, 119, 121
Jumna, river, 22, 28, 35, 37, 41, 43, 47, 48, 61, 74, 82, 85, pls. 8, 13-15

Kalidasa, Sanskrit poet, 73
Kalindi, a queen of Krishna, 57, 60, 64
Kaliya, giant hydra-headed snake, 35, 42, 46, 108, 116, pls. 8, 10 (comment)
Kaliyavana, 54
Kalpasutra, Jain Scripture, 96
Kama, god of passion, 18, 64
Kamalavati, mother of Radha, 72

INDEX

Kangra, Punjab Hills, 93, 108–11, pl. 3 (comment)
Kangra Painting, 109, 110, 121
Kangra Valley Painting, 121
Kanoria, Gopi Krishna, 9, pls. 7, 29, 39
Kansa, tyrant king of Mathura, son of Pavanarekha by the demon Drumalika, 26–9, 31, 33, 43–50, 54, 55, 57, 62, 110, 116, pls. 3, 9 (comment), 16 (comment), 17, 35 (comment)
Karna, leading Kaurava killed by Arjuna at Kurukshetra, 23
Kauravas, the 100 sons of Dhritarashtra, rivals of the Pandavas (vide *Mahabharata*), 20, 21, 23, 26, 51, 62, 66, 67
Kennings, Anglo-Saxon, 116
Keshav Das, poet, 84, 91, 99, 100, 105, pls. 28, 30 (comment)
Keshava, pseudonym for Krishna, 116
Kesi, horse demon, 44, 45, 115
Keyt, George, artist and translator of the *Gita Govinda*, 9, 76–83, 112, 113, 119, 121, pls. 21–7 (comments)
Khandalawala, Karl, 95, 96, pls. 10, 23 (comment)
Khurasan, 97, pl. 1 (comment)
Kirpal Pal, Raja of Basohli, 104, 105, 107, pl. 10 (comment)
Kishangarh, Rajasthan, 103, pl. 39
Kotah, Rajasthan, 103
Krishna Das, poet, 84
Kubera, yaksha king, pl. 5 (comment)
Kubja, hunchback girl, 47, 53, 54
Kulu, Punjab Hills, 107, 111
Kumbhan Das, poet, 84
Kundulpur, 56
Raja of, father of Rukmini, 55
Kunti, wife of Pandu, mother of the Pandavas, sister of Vasudeva (Krishna's father), 20, 21, 51, 57, 62, 64
Kuru, common ancestor of the Pandavas and Kauravas, 20
Kurukshetra, battlefield of, 15, 21, 26, 61
Kushala, Kangra artist, 110, pls. 3, 21, 36
Kuvara, brother of Nala, 32, pl. 5.

Lahore, State Museum, pl. 26
Lanka, modern Ceylon, 57
Léger, F., 112
Lewis, C. S., 119
Lohuizen, Dr. Joan van, de Leeuw, 120
Love Songs of Asia, 121
Lucknow, State Museum, pl. 5

MacNeice, Louis, 15
Madhu, demon, 116
Magadha, 26, 54, 55
Mahabharata, 11, 17, 19–25, 51, 70, 98, 115
Mahavira, founder of Jainism, 94
Malabar, 84
Malwa, Central India, 97, 100–2
Manaku, Basohli princess, patron of painting, 107, pl. 26 (comment)

Manohar, Mewar artist, 100
Marg, Indian art journal, 95, 103, 111, 117
Masterpieces of Rajput Painting, 104, 119, 121
Mathers, E. Powys, 121
Mathura, town in Northern India, 26, 29, 30, 38, 39, 44–55, 61, 74, 76, pls. 16 (comment), 17 (comment)
Mazumdar, M. R., 94
R. C., 115, 121
Mehendale, M. A., 115, 116
Mehta, N. C., 95, 107, 110, 121, pls. 4, 21, 22, 36
Mewar, Rajasthan, 100, 103
Mira Bai, poetess, 84
Mithila, 111
Modern Vernacular Literature of Hindustan, The, 121
Mody, J. K., pls. 3, 8, 11, 13, 15, 16
Monkey demon, 64
Mookerjee, A., 112
Moonlight, master of the, pls. 13–5
Moti Chandra, 96
Mukund, Mughal artist, pl. 2
Murari, pseudonym for Krishna, 116
Muru (or Mura), arch demon, 58, 117
Muslim artists, 99, 100
invasions, 73
rulers, 93, 96, 98
states, 97, 101
Mustaka, wrestler, 48

Nainsukh, Guler artist, pls. 3 (comment), 21 (comment)
Nala, brother of Kuvara, 32, pl. 5
Nanda, wealthy herdsman, foster-father of Krishna, 27–32, 35–41, 44–53, 61, 62, 77, 107, pls. 5, 10, 12, 20
Narada, sage, 60
Naraka, demon son of Earth, 58, 117
Nasiruddin, Mewar artist, 100
Nayikas and Nayakas, 90, 91, 102, pl. 28
New Delhi, National Museum, pls. 5, 9, 12, 14, 20, 28
New Testament, 15
Nihal Chand, Kishangarh artist, 103
Nude, the, pl. 11
Nurpur, Punjab Hills, 107, 111

Ocean, 69
Orchha, Central India, 84, 91, 99

Painting, Basohli, 104–7, pls. 4, 10, 18 (comment), 26 (comment), 27, 30, 31
Bengali, 111, 112
Bikaner, 99, 100
Bilaspur, 107, 111, pl. 18
Bundi, 101, 102, pls. 28, 32
Deccani, 97, pl. 34
European, pl. 1 (comment)
Flemish, 14
Garhwal, 107, 108, pls. 3 (comment), 7, 8 (comment), 12, 19, 20, 25, 35, 38 (comment)

125

Painting (*continued*)
  German, 93
  Gujarati, 94, 121
  Guler, 107, 108, 117, 121, pls. 3 (comment), 21 (comment), 37
  Italian, 14
  Jain, 94–6, pl. 22 (comment)
  Jaipur, 104, 120
  Jaunpur, 96, pls. 23, 24
  Kalighat, 111, 112
  Kangra, 93, 108–111, 117, 121, pls. 3, 5, 6, 8, 9, 11, 13–17, 21, 36
  Kishangarh, 103, 104, pl. 39
  Maithil, 111
  Malwa, 97, 101, 102, pl. 33
  Mughal, 13, 97–9, 103, 105, 107, 121, pls. 1, 2, 3 (comment)
  Nahan, pl. 38
  Persian, 97
  Udaipur, Mewar, 100, 101, 103–5, pl. 28 (comment), 29
  Western Indian, 94–6, pl. 22 (comment)
  Western Rajasthani, pl. 22
Panchala, kingdom of, 20, 21
Pandavas, five sons of Pandu, rivals of the Kauravas (vide *Mahabharata*), 20–6, 51, 57, 62–6, 70, 116
Pandu, second son of Kuru, father of the Pandavas, 20
Parasurama, 'Rama with the Axe,' incarnation of Vishnu, 20
Parikshit, great-grandson of Krishna, 69
Parmanand Das, poet, 84
Parvati, consort of Siva, 37
Pavanarekha, wife of King Ugrasena, 26
Prabhasa, town near Dwarka, 68, 94, pl. 1 (comment)
Prabhavananda, Swami, 15, 24, 116, 121
Pradyumna, Krishna's son by Rukmini, 64
Pragjyotisha, city of the demon, Naraka, 58, 117
Pralamba, demon in human form, 35, pls. 9, 10 (comment)
Pratap Singh, Raja of Jaipur, 104
Prince of Wales Museum, Bombay, pls. 23, 24, 32
Punjab Hills, 4, 13, 93, 98, 104, 105, 107, 111
Purkhu, Kangra artist, 109, 110, pls. 3, 5, 6. 8, 9, 11, 16
Putana, ogress, 29, 42

Radha, Krishna's chief cowgirl love, 15, 16, 72–90, 92, 96, 98, 103–5, 109–11, 113, 117, pls. 13 (comment), 20–29, 31–39
Ragas and *Raginis*, modes of Indian music, 84, 101, 102, 107, pls. 33, 34
Ragas and Raginis, 121
Raghavan, V., 120
Rajasthan, 13, 95, 96, 99–105
Rajput Painting (Coomaraswamy), 104, 108, 121, pl. 8 (comment)
  (Gray), 121

Ram Gopal, 15
Rama, incarnation of Vishnu, 20, 57, 115
Ramayana, 98
Rana Jagat Singh, ruler of Mewar, 100
Rana Raj Singh, ruler of Mewar, 100, 105
Randhawa, M. S., 121
Rasamanjari, Sanskrit treatise by Bhanu Datta, 9, 105, 106, 120, pls. 30, 31
Rasika Priya, Hindi treatise by Keshav Das, 11, 90–2, 99–102, 105, 120, pls. 28, 30 (comment)
Razmnama, Persian abridgement of the *Mahabharata*, 98, pls. 1, 2
Re-birth, theory of, 17–19
Revati, wife of Balarama, 55
Rohini, a wife of Vasudeva, mother of Balarama, 27–31, 35, 44, 53, 69
Roopa-lekha, Indian art journal, 121
Roy, Jamini, 112
Roy, P. C., 121
Rukma, brother of Rukmini, 56, 64
Rukmini, Krishna's first queen, 15, 55, 56, 59, 60, 64, 66, 69–72, 118, pl. 18
Ruknuddin, Bikaner artist, 99
Rupam, Indian art journal, 118
Russell, M., 113

Saktasura, demon, 30
Sankhasura, yaksha demon, 44
Sansar Chand, Raja of Kangra, 13, 108–11
Sat Sai, poems by Bihari Lal, 84, 110, pl. 36
Sattrajit, father of Satyabhama, 56, 57
Satyabhama, a queen of Krishna, 56, 57, 59, 60
Sawant Singh, Raja of Kishangarh, 103
Scroll paintings, 112
Sen, D. C., 121
Sen, R. N., 121
Sesha, serpent of eternity, a part of Vishnu, 27, 69, pl. 1
Shah Jahan, Mughal emperor, 99
Shahabaddin, Mewar artist, 100
Sher-Gil, Amrita, 112
Shiraz, 97
Sirmur, Punjab Hills, pl. 38 (comment)
Sisupala, claimant to Rukmini, rival of Krishna, 22, 56, 59, 66, pl. 18 (comment)
Sitwell, Sacheverell, 14
Siva, 17, 18, 37, 44, 47, 58, 59, 64, 65, 67, pl. 2
Srinagar, Garhwal, 108
St. John of the Cross, 74, 75
Stchoukine, I., 121
Studies in Indian Painting, 121
Subhadra, sister of Krishna, 22, 64, 65
Sudama, brahman, early friend of Krishna, 62, 63, 108, pl. 19
Sudarsana, celestial dancer, 40, 41
Sur Das, poet, 84, 86, pl. 29
Surabhi, cow of plenty, 40

INDEX

Sursagar, Hindi poem, pl. 29
Surya, sun god, 18

Tagore, Rabindranath, 112
Taking of Toll, The, 121
Ten Burnt Offerings, 15
Tess of the D'Urbervilles, 119
Trinavarta, whirlwind demon, 30.

Udaipur, chief city, Mewar, 100, 101, 103–5, pl. 29 (comment)
Udho, friend of Krishna, 52–4, 68
Ugrasena, king of Mathura, 26, 48, 54, 57, 67, 69
Ugrasura, snake demon, 33
Upanishads, 17
Usa, daughter of demon Vanasura, 64

Vaikuntha, heaven of Vishnu, 18, 59
Vallabhacharya, poet, 84
Vamana, dwarf incarnation of Vishnu, 20
Vanasura, demon with a thousand arms, 64
Varuna, god of water, 18, 38, pl. 1
Vasudeva, Yadava prince, father of Krishna, husband of Devaki, brother of Kunti, 21, 27–31, 44, 46, 48–53, 62, 69, pl. 3
Vatsasura, cow demon, 33
Vedas, 39, 46, 56, 117
Vedic Age, The, 121

Victoria and Albert Museum, 98, pls. 30, 33, 34
Vidyapati, poet, 84, 87, 89, 90, 111
Vishnu, 17–20, 26–9, 36, 39, 40, 45–7, 49, 56–8, 67, 69, 70, 76, 115, 116, pl. 2 (comment)
Vishnu Purana, 25, 116, 117, pl. 8 (comment)
Visvakarma, divine architect, 54, 63
Vrishabhanu, father of Radha, 72
Vrishnis, kinsmen of Krishna, 23
Vyamasura, wolf demon, 45

Wellesz, E., 98
Williams, R. H. B., pl. 30 (comment)
Wilson, H. H., 116, 117, 121
Winternitz, M., 121
Wonder that was India, The, 19, 115, 117, 121
Wrestlers, Krishna's conflict with, 44, 45, 48, pl. 17

Yadavas, pastoral caste, Krishna's castemen, 21, 26, 27, 45, 49–57, 61, 62, 64, 66–9, 117, pls. 1 (comment), 2 (comment)
Yasoda, wife of Nanda, foster-mother of Krishna, 27–33, 35, 49, 51–3, 61, 62, 72, 109
Yoga, 19, 23
Yudhisthira, leader of the Pandavas, husband of Draupadi, 21–3, 65, 66

THE PLATES

PLATE 1

The Death of Balarama

Illustration to the Persian abridgement of the
Mahabharata, the *Razmnama* (or Book of the Wars)
By Basawan
Mughal (Akbar period), c. 1595
Collection H.H. the Maharaja of Jaipur, Jaipur

Although illustrations of the Hindu epic, the *Mahabharata*, were rarely commissioned by Hindu patrons, the gigantic text possessed a unique appeal to Indian minds and for this reason the Mughal emperor, Akbar, chose it for translation into Persian. 'Having observed the fanatical hatred prevailing between Hindus and Muslims,' writes his biographer, Abul Fazl, 'and convinced that it arose only from their mutual ignorance, the enlightened monarch wished to dispel the same by rendering the books of the former accessible to the latter.' The work of translation was begun in 1582 and was probably concluded in 1588 when Abul Fazl wrote the preface. It is unlikely, however, that the illustrations were completed before 1595.

The present picture by one of Akbar's greatest Hindu artists illustrates the sensitive naturalism which from antecedents in Khurasan came to elegant maturity in Mughal India between 1585 and 1600. Certain details—the drapery with its shaded folds, the steeples rising in the distance—are modelled on the European Renaissance pictures which by 1580 had already reached the court. Other details such as the lithe squirrels gambolling in the tree, the rearing snakes and dense luxuriant foliage can only have been painted by an artist devoted to the Indian scene.

In subject, the picture represents what Krishna saw on his return from destroying the Yadavas at Prabhasa. Balarama, his half-brother, has gone down to the sea and has there yielded up his spirit. Sesha, the great serpent, who is part of Vishnu himself, is now issuing from the body—Balarama having been his incarnation. Snakes come to greet him while Varuna, the god of water, stands as 'an old man of the sea' ready to escort him to his long home.

PLATE 2

The Death of Krishna

Illustration to the Persian abridgement of the
Mahabharata, the *Razmnama* (or Book of the Wars)
By Mukund
Mughal (Akbar period), c. 1595
Collection H.H. the Maharaja of Jaipur, Jaipur

Following the death of Balarama, Krishna prepares to leave the world. He sits in meditation and is shot in the sole of his right foot by Jara, a Bhil hunter—the arrow which kills him being tipped with part of the iron which has caused the destruction of the Yadavas.

The picture shows Krishna reclining on a platform of the kind still constructed in India at the base of sacred trees. An arrow transfixes his right foot while the hunter, dressed as a courtier in Mughal dress, is shown releasing the bow. In front of Krishna stand four awe-struck figures, representing the celestial sages and devotees of Vishnu who have come to attend his passing. In the sky four gods look down. To the right is Siva. Then, a little to the left, is four-headed Brahma, below him, Indra, his body spotted with a thousand eyes and finally a fourth god of uncertain identity. Around the platform surges the snarling sea as if impatiently awaiting Krishna's death before engulfing the doomed Dwarka.

The painting is by a colleague of Basawan (Plate 1) and illustrates the same great text.

PLATE 3

The Slaughter of an Innocent

Illustration to the *Bhagavata Purana*
Kangra, Punjab Hills, *c.* 1790
J. K. Mody collection, Bombay

Following the expansion of Indian miniature painting in the early seventeenth century, illustrated versions of the tenth book of the *Bhagavata Purana* began to be produced in parts of Hindu India. It was in the Punjab Hills, at the end of the eighteenth century, however, that romance and religion achieved their most delicate expression. The artist chiefly responsible was a certain Nainsukh who had arrived at the State of Guler in about 1740. His way of painting had marked affinities with that of Basawan (Plate 1) and represents a blend of early Mughal naturalism with later Hindu sentiment. The style founded by him influenced members of his own family, including his nephew Kushala and ultimately spread to Kangra and Garhwal where it reached its greatest heights. The present picture, together with Plates 5, 6, 8, 9, 11 and 16, is possibly by the Kangra artist Purkhu and with others of the series illustrates perhaps the greatest interpretation of the *Bhagavata Purana* ever produced in Indian painting.

In the picture, the tyrant ruler Kansa is sleeping on a bed as a courtier prepares to break the fateful news of Krishna's birth. To the right, Devaki, Krishna's mother, nurses the baby girl whom her husband, Vasudeva, has substituted for the infant Krishna. Kansa is wresting the baby from her in order to dash its head against a boulder. As he does so, she eludes his grasp and ascends to heaven in a flash, being, in fact, the eight-armed goddess Devi.

PLATE 4

Krishna stealing Butter

Illustration to an incident from the *Bhagavata Purana*
Basohli, Punjab Hills, *c.* 1700
N. C. Mehta collection, Bombay

Besides illustrating the tenth book of the *Bhagavata Purana* as a whole, Indian artists sometimes chose isolated episodes and composed their pictures around them. The present picture is an instance of this practice, its subject being the baby Krishna pilfering butter. As Yasoda, Krishna's foster-mother, goes inside the house, Krishna and the cowherd children stage an impudent raid. A cowherd boy mounts a wooden mortar and then, balanced on his shoulders, the young Krishna helps himself to the butter which is kept stored in a pot suspended by strings from the roof. A second cowherd boy reaches up to lift the butter down while edging in from the right, a monkey, emblematic of mischievous thieving, shares in the spoil.

The picture illustrates the wild and vehemently expressive style of painting which suddenly appeared at Basohli, a tiny State in the Punjab Hills, towards the end of the seventeenth century. The jagged form of Yasoda, cut in two by the lintel of the doorway, the stabbing lines of the churning pole, grazing sticks and corcs, as well as the sharp angles of the house and its furniture, all contribute to a state of taut excitement.

PLATE 5

The Felling of the Trees

Illustration to the *Bhagavata Purana*
Kangra, Punjab Hills, *c.* 1790
State Museum, Lucknow

From the same great series as Plate 3, here attributed to the Kangra artist Purkhu.

The young Krishna, tied to a mortar to keep him out of mischief, has dragged it between two trees and thereby uprooted them. The cowherds, led by the bearded Nanda, Krishna's foster-father, have hurried to the scene and Balarama, Krishna's half-brother, is excitedly pointing out that Krishna is safe. In the foreground, emerging from the earth are two crowned figures—Nala and Kuvara, the sons of the yaksha king, Kubera, who, as a consequence of a curse had been turned into the two trees. Doomed to await Krishna's intervention, they have now been released. Reclining on the trunks, still tied to the mortar, the young Krishna surveys the scene with pert satisfaction.

PLATE 6

The Road to Brindaban

Illustration to the *Bhagavata Purana*
Kangra, Punjab Hills, *c.* 1790
National Museum, New Delhi

With Plates 3 and 5, part of the series attributed to Purkhu.

Led by Nanda, the majestic figure in the front bullock-cart, the cowherds are moving a day's march across the River Jumna to enjoy the larger freedom of Brindaban. Their possessions—bundles of clothes, spinning-wheels, baskets of grain and pitchers—are being taken with them and mounted with Yasoda on a second cart go the children, Balarama and Krishna. With its great variety of stances, simple naturalism and air of innocent calm, the picture exactly expresses the terms of tender familiarity on which the cowherds lived with Krishna.

PLATE 7

Krishna milking

Illustration to the *Bhagavata Purana*
Garhwal, Punjab Hills, *c.* 1800
G. K. Kanoria collection, Calcutta

Like Plate 4, an illustration of an isolated episode. Krishna, having graduated from tending the calves, is milking a cow, his mind filled with brooding thoughts. A cowgirl restrains the calf by tugging at its string while the cow licks its restive offspring with tender care. Other details—the tree clasped by a flowering creeper, the peacock perched in its branches—suggest the cowgirls' growing love. The image of tree and creeper was a common symbol in poetry for the lover embraced by his beloved and peacocks, thirsting for rain, were evocative of desire.

In style, the picture represents the end of the first great phase of Garhwal painting (*c.* 1770–1804) when romantic themes were treated with glowing ardour.

PLATE 8

The Quelling of the Snake Kaliya

Illustration to the *Bhagavata Purana*
Kangra, Punjab Hills, *c.* 1790
J. K. Mody collection, Bombay

With Plates 3, 5 and 6, an example of Kangra painting in its most serene form.

Krishna, having defied the hydra-headed snake whose poison has befouled the River Jumna, is dancing in triumph on its sagging heads. The snake's consorts plead for mercy—one of them holding out bunches of lotus flowers, the others folding their hands or stretching out their arms in mute entreaty. The river is once again depicted as a surging flood but it is the master-artist's command of sinuous line and power of suffusing a scene of turmoil with majestic calm which gives the picture greatness.

Although the present study is true to the *Bhagavata Purana* where the snake is explicitly described as vacatingt he water and meeting its end on dry land, other pictures, notably those from Garhwal[1] follow the *Vishnu Purana* and show the final struggle taking place in the river itself.

[1] Reproduced A. K. Coomaraswamy, *Rajput Painting* (Oxford, 1916), Vol. II, Plates 53 and 54.

PLATE 9

Balarama killing the Demon Pralamba

Illustration to the *Bhagavata Purana*
Kangra, Punjab Hills, *c.* 1790
National Museum, New Delhi

A further example from the Kangra series, here attributed to Purkhu.

As part of his war on Krishna and young boys, the tyrant Kansa sends various demons to harry and kill them, the present picture showing four stages in one such attack. To the right, the cowherd children, divided into two parties, face each other by an ant-hill, Krishna with arms crossed heading the right-hand group and Balarama the left. Concealed as a cowherd in Krishna's party, the demon Pralamba awaits an opportunity of killing Balarama. The second stage, in the right-hand bottom corner, shows Balarama's party giving the other side 'pick-a-backs,' after having been vanquished in a game of guessing flowers and fruit. The third stage is reached in the top left-hand corner. Here Pralamba has regained his demon form and is hurrying off with Balarama. Balarama's left hand is tightly clutched but with his right he beats at the demon's head. The fourth and final stage is illustrated in the bottom left-hand corner where Balarama has subdued the demon and is about to slay him.

The picture departs from the normal version, as given in the *Bhagavata Purana*, by showing Balarama's side, instead of Krishna's, carrying out the forfeits. According to the *Purana*, it was Krishna's side that lost and since Pralamba was among the defeated, he was in a position to take Balarama for a ride. It is likely, however, that in view of the other episode in the *Purana* in which Krishna humbles his favourite cowgirl when she asks to be carried (Plate 14), the artist shrank from showing Krishna in this servile posture so changed the two sides round.

PLATE 10

The Forest Fire

Illustration to an incident from the *Bhagavata Purana*
Basohli, Punjab Hills *c.* 1680
Karl Khandalavala collection, Bombay

Under Raja Kirpal Pal (*c.* 1680–1693), painting at Basohli attained a savage intensity of expression—the present picture illustrating the style in its earliest and greatest phase. Surrounded by a ring of fire and with cowherd boys and cattle stupefied by smoke, Krishna is putting out the blaze by sucking the flames into his cheeks. Deer and pig are bounding to safety while birds and wild bees hover distractedly overhead.

During his life among the cowherds, Krishna was on two occasions confronted with a forest fire—the first, on the night following his struggle with Kaliya the snake when Nanda, Yasoda and other cowherds and cowgirls were also present and the second, following Balarama's encounter with the demon Pralamba (Plate 10), when only cowherd boys were with him. Since Nanda and the cowgirls are absent from the present picture, it is probably the second of these two occasions which is illustrated.

For a reproduction in colour of this passionately glowing picture, see Karl Khandalavala, *Indian Sculpture and Painting* (Bombay, 1938) (Plate 10).

PLATE 11

The Stealing of the Clothes

Illustration to the *Bhagavata Purana*
Kangra, Punjab Hills, *c.* 1790
J. K. Mody collection, Bombay

Despite the Indian delight in sensuous charm, the nude was only rarely depicted in Indian painting—feelings of reverence and delicacy forbidding too unabashed a portrayal of the feminine physique. The present picture with its band of nude girls is therefore an exception—the facts of the *Purana* rendering necessary their frank inclusion.

The scene illustrated concerns the efforts of the cowgirls to win Krishna's love. Bathing naked in the river at dawn in order to rid themselves of sin, they are surprised by Krishna who takes their clothes up into a tree. When they beg him to return them, he insists that each should freely expose herself before him, arguing that only in this way can they convince him of their love. In the picture, the girls are shyly advancing while Krishna looks down at them from the tree.

PLATE 12

The Raising of Mount Govardhana

Illustration to an incident from the *Bhagavata Purana*
Garhwal, Punjab Hills, *c.* 1790
National Museum, New Delhi

With Plate 7, an example of Garhwal painting and its use of smoothly curving line.

Krishna is lifting Mount Govardhana on his little finger and Nanda, the cowherds and cowgirls are sheltering underneath. The occasion is Krishna's slight to Indra, king of the gods and lord of the clouds, whose worship he has persuaded the cowherds to abandon. Incensed at Krishna's action, Indra has retaliated by sending storms of rain.

In the picture, Indra, a tiny figure mounted on a white elephant careers across the sky, goading the clouds to fall in torrents. Lightning flickers wildly and on Govardhana itself, the torn and shattered trees bespeak the gale's havoc. Below all is calm as the cowherds acclaim Krishna's power.

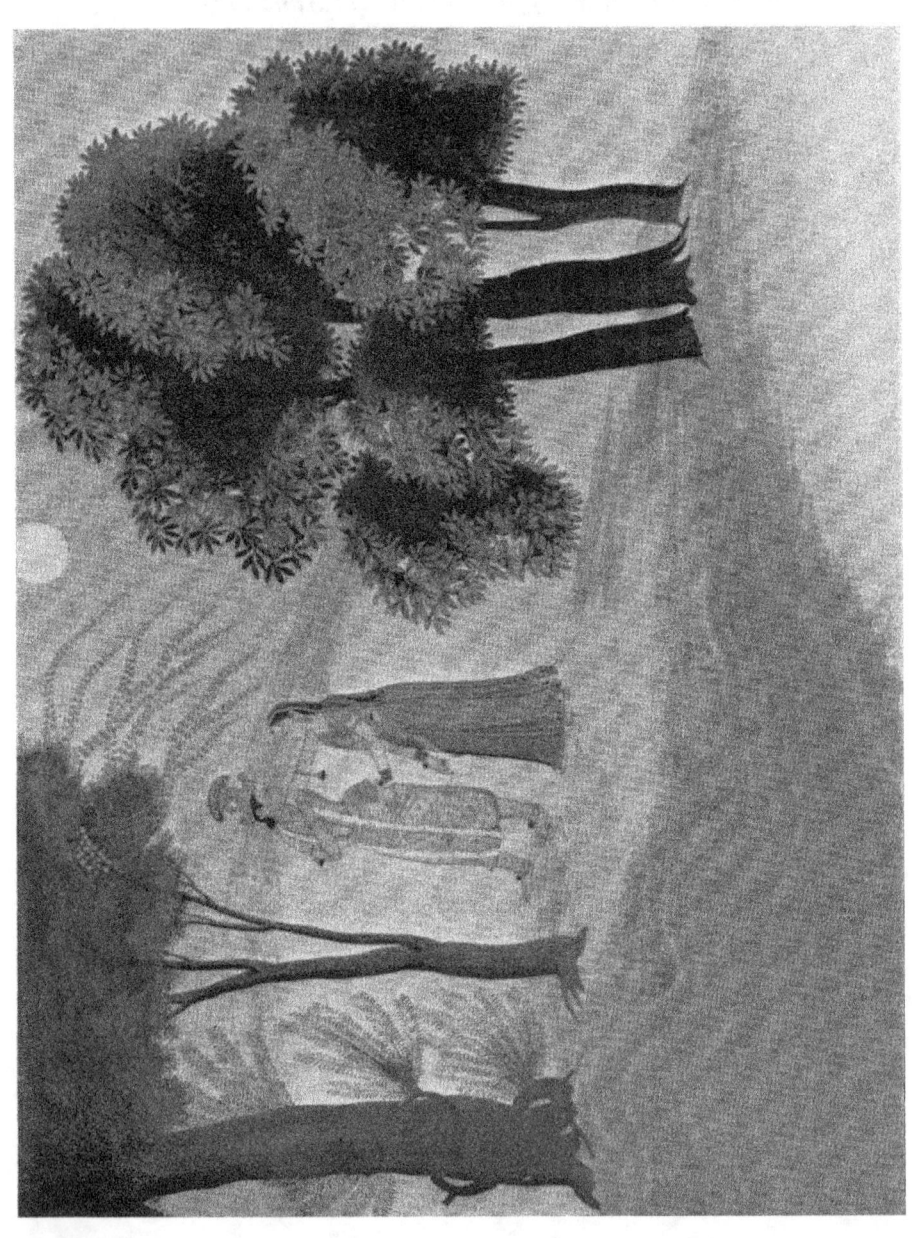

PLATE 13

Krishna with his Favourite after leaving the Dance

Illustration to the *Bhagavata Purana*
Kangra, Punjab Hills, *c.* 1790
J. K. Mody collection, Bombay

Besides Purkhu, at least two other master-artists worked at Kangra towards the end of the eighteenth century—one, responsible for the present picture and Plates 14 and 15, being still unknown. He is here referred to as 'the master of the moonlight' on account of his special preoccupation with moonlight effects.

The present picture shows Krishna and a girl standing by an inlet of the River Jumna. The girl is later to be identified as Radha but in the *Bhagavata Purana* she is merely referred to as one who has been particularly favoured, her actual name being suppressed. The moment is some time after they have left the circular dance and before their sudden separation. Krishna, whose hand rests on the girl's shoulder, is urging her forward but the girl is weary and begs him to carry her. The incident illustrates one of the vicissitudes in Radha and Krishna's romance and was later to be endowed with deep religious meaning.

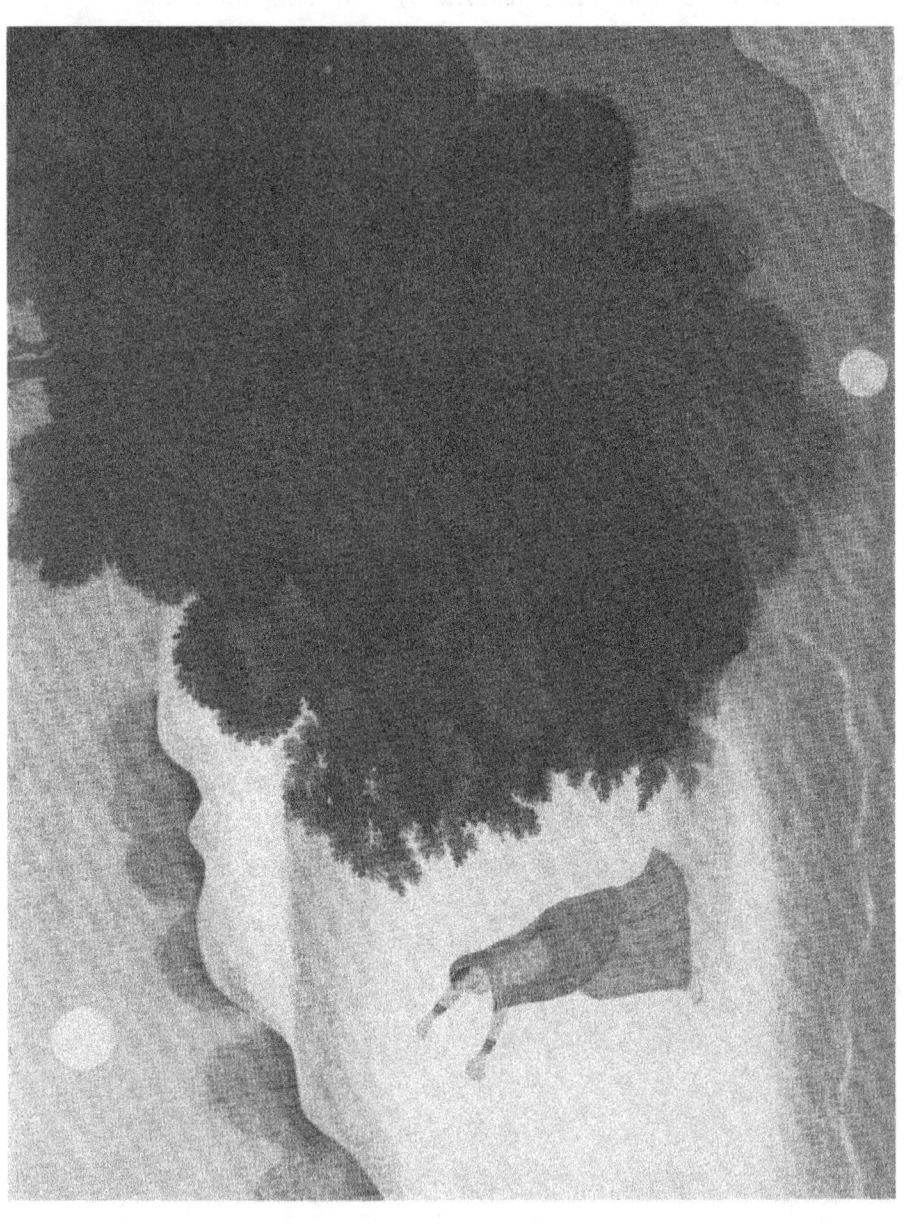

PLATE 14

Krishna's Favourite deserted

Illustration to the *Bhagavata Purana*
Kangra, Punjab Hills, *c.* 1790
National Museum, New Delhi

From the same series as Plates 13 and 15 by 'the master of the moonlight.'

The girl's request (Plate 13) that Krishna should carry her brings to a head the question of Krishna's proper status. To an adoring lover, the request is not unreasonable. Made to God, it implies an excess of pride. Despite their impassioned love-making, therefore, the girl must be humbled and as she puts out her arms and prepares to mount, Krishna vanishes.

In the picture, the great woods overhanging the rolling Jumna are tilting forward as if to join the girl in her agonized advances while around her rise the bleak and empty slopes, their eerie loneliness intensified by frigid moonlight.

PLATE 15

The Quest for Krishna

Illustration to the *Bhagavata Purana*
Kangra, Punjab Hills, *c.* 1790
J. K. Mody collection, Bombay

By the same 'master of the moonlight' as Plates 13 and 14.

Krishna's favourite, stunned by his brusque desertion, has now been met by a party of cowgirls. Their plight is similar to her own, for, after enjoying his enchanting love, they also have been deserted when Krishna left the dance taking his favourite with him. In the picture, Radha holds her head in anguish while to the right the cowgirls look at her in mute distress. Drooping branches echo their stricken love while a tree in the background, its branches stretching wanly against the sky, suggests their plaintive yearning.

PLATE 16

The Eve of the final Encounter

Illustration to the *Bhagavata Purana*
Kangra, Punjab Hills, *c.* 1790
J. K. Mody collection, Bombay

From the same series as Plates 3, 5, 6, 8, 9 and 11, here attributed to the Kangra artist Purkhu.

Invited by Kansa, the tyrant king, to attend a festival of arms, Nanda and the cowherds have arrived at Mathura and pitched their tents outside the walls. Krishna and Balarama are eating their evening meal by candle-light, a cowherd, wearing a dark cloak to keep off the night air, is attending to the bullocks while three cowherd boys, worn out by the day's march, rest on string-beds under the night sky. In the background, Krishna and Balarama, having finished their meal, are peacefully sleeping, serenely indifferent to the struggle which awaits them the next day. The moon waning in the sky parallels the tyrant's declining fortunes.

PLATE 17

The End of the Tyrant

Illustration to the *Bhagavata Purana*
Kangra, Punjab Hills, c. 1790
Chester Beatty Library, Dublin

In the same style as Plate 16, but perhaps from a different series.

The festival of arms is now in progress but has already taken an unexpected turn. Set on by the savage elephant, Krishna and Balarama have killed it and taken out the tusks. They have then engaged two giant wrestlers, Krishna killing his opponent outright. In the picture Balarama is about to kill the other wrestler and Krishna, holding an elephant tusk under his arm, looks at the king with calm defiance. The king's end is now in sight for a little later Krishna will spring on the platform and hurl him to his death. Gathered in the wide arena, townspeople from Mathura await the outcome, while cowherd boys delightedly encourage the two heroes.

PLATE 18

The Rape of Rukmini

Illustration to the *Bhagavata Purana*
Bilaspur, Punjab Hills, *c.* 1745
British Museum, London

Compared with Krishna's life among the cowherds, his adventures as a prince were only scantily illustrated in Indian painting—his consort Rukmini being totally eclipsed in courtly favour by the adored cowgirl, Radha. The present picture—one of the very few to represent the theme—shows Rukmini and her maids worshipping at the shrine to Devi, the earth mother, on the morning of her wedding. Her proposed husband is Sisupala and already he and his party have arrived to claim her hand. In despair Rukmini has apprised Krishna of her fate but does not know that he will intervene. As she worships, Krishna suddenly appears, places her on his chariot and, in the teeth of Sisupala's forces, carries her away. The picture illustrates the dramatic moment when after descending on the shrine, Krishna effects her rescue.

The picture is in an eighteenth-century style of painting which, from antecedents in Kashmir and the Punjab Plains, developed at Bilaspur. This small Rajput State adjoined Guler in the Punjab Hills and shared in the general revival of painting caused by the diffusion of artists from Basohli.

PLATE 19

Krishna welcoming the Brahman Sudama

Illustration to the Sudama episode in the *Bhagavata Purana*
Garhwal, Punjab Hills, c. 1785
Chester Beatty Library, Dublin

Sudama is a poor Brahman whose devotion leads him to go to Dwarka, and seek out Krishna. Krishna remembers the time when they had shared the same preceptor and warmly welcomes him to his princely palace. The picture shows Sudama in rags seated on a stool while Krishna washes his feet and hails him as a Brahman. In close attendance are various ladies of the court, their graceful forms transcribed with sinuous delicacy and suave poetic charm.

Although an episode in Krishna's later career as a prince and one designed to buttress the priestly caste of Brahmans, the story—with its emphasis on loving devotion—is actually in close accord with Krishna's life among the cowherds. For this reason, it probably continued to excite interest long after other aspects of his courtly life had been ignored. In this respect, Sudama's visit to Krishna is as much a parable of divine love as Krishna's dances with the cowgirls.

PLATE 20

The Beginnings of Romance

Illustration to the *Gita Govinda*
Garhwal, Punjab Hills, *c.* 1790
National Museum, New Delhi

The first poem to celebrate Radha as Krishna's supreme love is the *Gita Govinda* of Jayadeva, written at the end of the twelfth century. The poem recounts Radha's anguish at Krishna's fickleness, his subsequent repentance and finally their passionate re-union.

The present picture with its glamorous interpretation of the forest in spring illustrates the poem's opening verse and re-creates the setting in terms of which the drama will proceed. Nanda, the tall figure towering above the cowherd children, is commanding Radha to take Krishna home. The evening sky is dark with clouds, the wind has risen and already the flower-studded branches are swaying and bending in the breeze. Krishna is still a young boy and Radha a girl a few years older. As Radha takes him home, they loiter by the river, passion suddenly flares and they fall into each other's arms. In this way, the verse declares, the loves of Radha and Krishna began. The left-hand side of the picture shows the two lovers embracing—the change in their attitudes being reflected in their altered heights. Krishna who originally was shorter than Radha is now the taller of the two, the change suggesting the mature character of their passionate relations.

The picture with its graceful feminine forms and twining lines has the same quality of rhythmical exaltation as Plates 19 and 35, a quality typical of the Garwhal master-artist in his greatest phase.

PLATE 21

Krishna playing on the Flute

Illustration to the *Gita Govinda*
Kangra, Punjab Hills, c. 1790
N. C. Mehta collection, Bombay

As Radha wilts in lonely anguish, a friend describes how Krishna is behaving.

'The wife of a certain herdsman sings as Krishna sounds a tune of love
Krishna here disports himself with charming women given to love.'

In the picture, Radha sits beneath a flowering tree, conversing with the friend while, to the right, Krishna plays the flute to a circle of adoring girls.

The painting is by a Kangra master, perhaps Kushala, the nephew of the Guler artist, Nainsukh, and illustrates the power of Kangra painters to imbue with innocent delicacy the most intensely emotional of situations. It was the investment of passion with dignity which was one of the chief contributions of Kangra painting to Indian art.

PLATE 22

Krishna dancing with the Cowgirls

Illustration to the *Gita Govinda*
Western Rajasthan, *c.* 1610
N. C. Mehta collection, Bombay

Besides describing Krishna's flute-playing, Radha's friend gives her an account of his love-making.

'An artless woman looks with ardour on Krishna's lotus face.'
'Another on the bank of the Jumna, when Krishna goes to a bamboo thicket,
Pulls at his garment to draw him back, so eager is she for amorous play.'
'Krishna praises another woman, lost with him in the dance of love,
The dance where the sweet low flute is heard in the clamour of bangles on hands that clap. He embraces one woman, he kisses another, and fondles another beautiful one.'
'Krishna here disports himself with charming women given to love.'

The present picture illustrates phases of this glamorous love-making—Krishna embracing one woman, dancing with another and conversing with a third. The background is a diagram of the forest as it might appear in spring—the slack looseness of treatment befitting the freedom of conduct adumbrated by the verse. The large insects hovering in the branches are the black bees of Indian love-poetry whose quest for flowers was regarded as symbolic of urgent lovers pestering their mistresses. In style the picture illustrates the Jain painting of Western India after its early angular rigidity had been softened by application to tender and more romantic themes.

PLATE 23

Krishna seated with the Cowgirls

Illustration to the *Gita Govinda*
Jaunpur, Eastern India, *c.* 1590
Prince of Wales Museum, Bombay

After flute-playing and dancing (Plates 21 and 22), Krishna sits with the cowgirls.

'With his limbs, tender and dark like rows of clumps of blue lotus flowers,
By herd girls surrounded, who embrace at pleasure any part of his body,
Friend, in spring, beautiful Krishna plays like Love's own self
Conducting the love sport, with love for all, bringing delight into being.'

And it is here that Radha finds him.

'May the smiling captivating Krishna protect you, whom Radha, blinded by love,
Violently kissed as she made as if singing a song of welcome saying,
"Your face is nectar, excellent," ardently clasping his bosom
In the presence of the fair-browed herdgirls dazed in the sport of love.'

The picture shows Krishna surrounded by a group of cowgirls, one of whom is caressing his leg. To the right, Radha and the friend are approaching through the trees. The style with its sharp curves and luxuriating smartness illustrates a vital development of the Jain manner in the later sixteenth century.[1]

[1] For a first discussion of this important series, see a contribution by Karl Khandalavala, 'A *Gita Govinda* Series in the Prince of Wales Museum,' *Bulletin of the Prince of Wales Museum, Bombay* (1956), No. 4.

PLATE 24

The neglected Radha

Illustration to the *Gita Govinda*
Jaunpur, Eastern India, *c.* 1590
Prince of Wales Museum, Bombay

Following his revels with the cowgirls, Krishna is smitten with remorse. He roams the forest, searching for the lovely Radha but finding her nowhere. As he pursues his quest, he encounters the friend and learns of Radha's dejected state.

'Her body is wholly tormented by the heat of the flame of desire;
But only of you, so loved, she thinks in her languour,
Your extinguishing body; secluded she waits, all wasted—
A short while, perhaps, surviving she lives. Formerly even a moment
   when weary she closed her eyes.
The moment's parting she could not endure, from the sight of you;
And now in this long separation, O how does she breathe
Having seen the flowery branch of the mango, the shaft of Love?'

In the picture, Radha is sitting in the forest, lonely and neglected. Trees surround her, suggesting by their rank luxuriance the upward surge of spring while cranes, slowly winging their way in pairs across the blackening sky, poignantly remind her of her former love.

PLATE 25

Krishna repentant

Illustration to the *Gita Govinda*
Garhwal, Punjab Hills, *c.* 1790

Learning of Radha's plight, Krishna longs to comfort her. Before approaching her, however, he spends a night passionately dallying with another cowgirl and only in the morning tenders his submission. By this time, Radha's mood has turned to bitter anger and although Krishna begs to be forgiven, Radha tells him to return to his latest love.

'Go, Krishna, go. Desist from uttering these deceitful words.
Follow her, you lotus-eyed, she who can dispel your trouble, go to her.'

In the picture, Krishna is striving to calm her ruffled feelings while Radha, 'cruel to one who loves you, unbending to one who bows, angry with one who desires, averting your face from this your lover,' has none of him.

According to the poem, the scene of this tense encounter is not a palace terrace but the forest—the Garhwal artist deeming a courtly setting more appropriate for Radha's exquisite physique. The suavely curving linear rhythm, characteristic of Garhwal painting at its best, is once again the means by which a mood of still adoration is sensitively conveyed.

PLATE 26

The last Tryst

Illustration to the *Gita Govinda*
Basohli, Punjab Hills, 1730
State Museum, Lahore

Having brusquely dismissed Krishna, Radha is overcome with longing and when he once again approaches her she showers on him her adoring love. The friend urges her to delay no longer.

'Your friends are all aware that you are ready for love's conflict
Go, your belt aloud with bells, shameless, amorous, to the meeting.'

Radha succumbs to her advice and slowly approaches Krishna's forest bower.

In the picture, Krishna is impatiently awaiting her while Radha, urged onward by the friend, pauses for a moment to shed her shyness. The picture is part of an illustrated edition of the poem executed in Basohli in 1730 for a local princess, the lady Manaku. As in other Basohli paintings, trees are shown as small and summary symbols, the horizon is a streak of clouds and there is a deliberate shrinkage from physical refinement. The purpose of the picture is rather to express with the maximum of power the savagery of passion and the stark nature of lovers' encounters.

PLATE 27

The closing Scene

Illustration to the *Gita Govinda*
Basohli, Punjab Hills, 1730
Art Gallery, Chandigarh, East Punjab

From the same series as Plate 26.
After agonies of 'love unsatisfied,' Radha and Krishna are at last reconciled.

> 'She looked on Krishna who desired only her, on him who for long wanted dalliance,
> Whose face with his pleasure was overwhelmed and who was possessed with Desire,
> Who engendered passion with his face made lovely through tremblings of glancing eyes,
> Like a pond in autumn with a pair of wagtails at play in a full-blown lotus.
> Like the gushing of the shower of sweat in the effort of her travel to come to his hearing,
> Radha's eyes let fall a shower of tears when she met her beloved,
> Tears of delight which went to the ends of her eyes and fell on her flawless necklace.
> When she went near the couch and her friends left the bower, scratching their faces to hide their smiles,
> And she looked on the mouth of her loved one, lovely with longing, under the power of love,
> The modest shame of that deer-eyed one departed.'

In the picture, Radha and Krishna are again united. Krishna has drawn Radha to him and is caressing her cheek while friends of Radha gossip in the courtyard. As in Plate 25, the artist has preferred a house to the forest—the sharp thrust of the angular walls exactly expressing the fierceness of the lovers' desires.

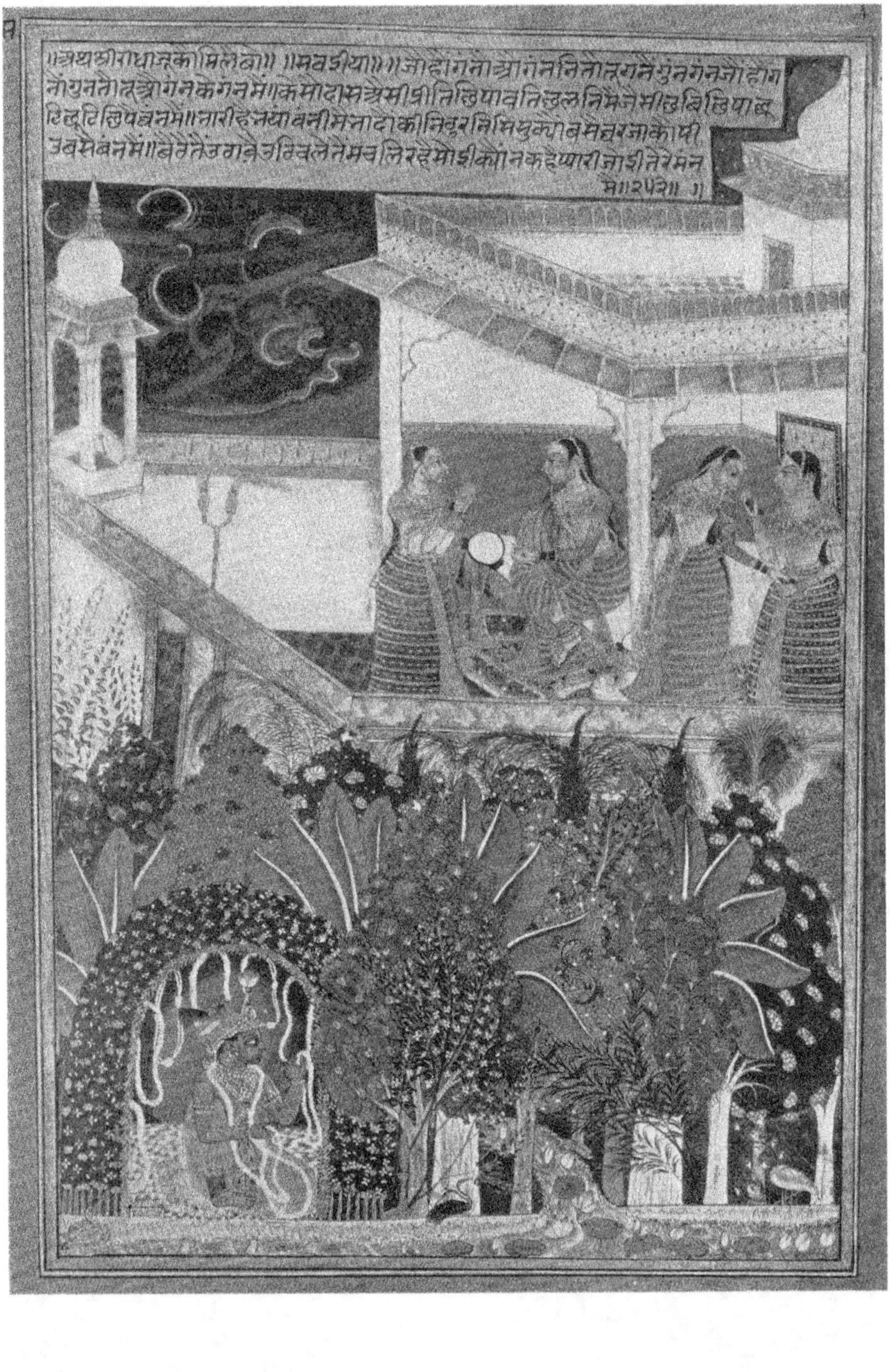

PLATE 28

Krishna awaiting Radha

Illustration to the *Rasika Priya* of Keshav Das
Bundi (Rajasthan), *c.* 1700
National Museum, New Delhi

Following the Sanskrit practice of discussing poetic taste, Keshav Das produced in 1592 a Hindi manual of poetics. In this book, poems on love were analysed with special reference to Krishna—Krishna himself sustaining the role of *nayaka* or ideal lover. During the seventeenth century, illustrated versions of the manual were produced—poems appearing at the top of the picture and the subjects being illustrated beneath. The present picture treats Radha as the *nayika* or ideal mistress and shows her about to visit Krishna. She is, at first, seated on a bed but, a little later, is leaning against a pillar as a maid or friend induces her to descend. In the left-hand bottom corner, Krishna sits quietly waiting. The bower is hung with garlands and floored with lotus petals while lightning twisting in the sky and torches flickering in the courtyard suggest the storm of love. The figures with their neat line and eager faces are typical of Bundi painting after it had broken free from the parent style of Udaipur.

PLATE 29

Radha and Krishna making Love

Illustration to the *Sursagar* of Sur Das
Udaipur, Rajasthan, *c.* 1650
G. K. Kanoria collection, Calcutta

Like Plate 28, an illustration to a Hindi poem analysing Krishna's conduct as ideal lover.

Krishna is here embracing Radha while outside two of Radha's friends await the outcome. Above them, two girls are watching peacocks—the strained advances of the birds and the ardent gazes of the girls hinting at the tense encounter proceeding in the room below.

The Udaipur style of painting with its vehement figures, geometrical compositions and brilliant colouring was admirably suited to interpreting scenes of romantic violence.

PLATE 30

The Lover approaching

Illustration to the *Rasamanjari* of Bhanu Datta
Basohli, Punjab Hills, c. 1680
Victoria and Albert Museum, London (I.S. 52-1953)

Although the *Rasika Priya* of Keshav Das was the manual of poetry most frequently illustrated by Indian artists, an earlier Sanskrit treatise, the *Rasamanjari* of Bhanu Datta, excited a particular raja's interest and resulted in the production at Basohli of a vividly illustrated text. The original poem discusses the conventions of ordinary lovers. Under this Basohli ruler's stimulus, however, the lover was deemed to be Krishna and although the verses make no allusion to him, it is Krishna who monopolizes the illustrations.

In the present instance, Krishna the lover, carrying a lotus-bud, is about to visit his mistress. The lady sits within, a pair of lotus-leaves protecting her nude bust, her hair falling in strands across her thighs. A maid explains to Krishna that her mistress is still at her toilet and chides him for arriving so abruptly.

The poem expresses the sentiments which a lover, denied early access, might fittingly address to his mistress.

'Longing to behold your path, my inmost heart—like a lotus-leaf when a new rain-cloud has appeared—mounts to your neck. My eye, too, takes wing, soaring in the guise of a lotus-bird, to regard the moon of your face.'[1]

In the picture, the lotus imagery is retained but is given a subtle twist—the lotus-leaves themselves, rather than the lover's inmost heart, being shown as mounting to the lady's neck.

[1] Translation R. H. B. Williams.

PLATE 31

Radha extinguishing the Lamp

Basohli, Punjab Hills, *c.* 1690
Bharat Kala Bhawan, Benares

Although no inscription has so far been published, it is likely that this picture is an illustration to the *Rasamanjari* of Bhanu Datta. The lover is once again Krishna and the girl most probably Radha. Krishna is inviting her to extinguish the lamp so that they may better enjoy the excitements of darkness.

With its air of violent frenzy, the picture is typical of Basohli painting at the end of the seventeenth century—the girl's wide-flung legs and rushing movements symbolizing the frantic nature of passionate desire.

PLATE 32

The Month of Asarh (June–July)

Illustration to a *Barahmasa* (or Cycle of the Months)
Bundi, Rajasthan, *c.* 1750
Prince of Wales Museum, Bombay

In Hindi poetry, lovers were sometimes described against a background of the twelve months—each month suggesting a different kind of mood or behaviour. Such poems known as *Barahmasa* (barah, twelve; masa, month) were sometimes illustrated—a princely lover and his lady being shown seated on a terrace with the sights and scenes appropriate to the month going on around. When this lover was identified with Krishna, any aspect of love was regarded as, in some degree, expressive of his character.

The present picture portrays the beginning of the Rains. The sky is black with clouds. On a lake lovers dally in a tiny pavilion, while in the background two princes consult a hermit before leaving on their travels. The rainy season was associated in poetry with love in separation and for this reason a lonely girl is shown walking in a wood. In a garden pavilion Krishna dallies with Radha, the approaching rain augmenting their desire.

PLATE 33

Radha and Krishna swinging

Illustration to the musical mode, *Hindola Raga*
('the swinging music')
Malwa, Middle India, c. 1750
Victoria and Albert Museum, London

A poem celebrating one of the main modes of Indian music is here represented by Radha and Krishna seated on a swing. The mode itself is called 'the swinging music' but since swinging was symbolical of love-making and also took place during the rains, the season of longing, its spirit was sometimes impersonated not by an ordinary prince but by Krishna himself. In the picture, peacocks, which were common symbols for the lover, are shown against a storm-tossed sky—the battered clouds and writhing lightning being symbolic references to 'the strife of love.' At the foot, lotus plants, their flowers symbolizing the male, their leaves the female, rise from a rain-filled river.

The picture represents one of the more poetic traditions of Indian painting but at a comparatively late stage of its development. During the sixteenth century the Malwa style had played a decisive part in the evolution of Rajput painting, but by the eighteenth century had shed something of its early ardour.

PLATE 34

Krishna attended by Ladies

Illustration to the musical mode, *Bhairava Raga*
Hyderabad, Deccan, *c.* 1750
Victoria and Albert Museum, London

Like Plate 33, an illustration to a poem accompanying a leading mode of Indian music. Krishna is sitting on a bed while Radha is rubbing his right arm with sandal preparatory to making love. In the foreground a maid is grinding the sandalwood into a paste. Although the poem itself contains no mention of Krishna, it speaks of Bhairava—a form of Siva—as a raging lover, 'insensate in a whirlwind of desire.' On this account Krishna—identified by his blue skin—has been inserted in the picture, his character as a lover according with the frenzied character of the poem. In the background a bullock is lifting water from a well and a gardener is bending over a bed of poppies. Ducks and fishes sport in the water.

Illustrations to modes of music were common features of the Muslim art of the Deccan—the association of certain modes with Krishna being carefully preserved. One of the finest series of *raga* and *ragini* pictures executed at Hyderabad and now in the India Office Library, London, contains exquisite versions with Krishna themes.

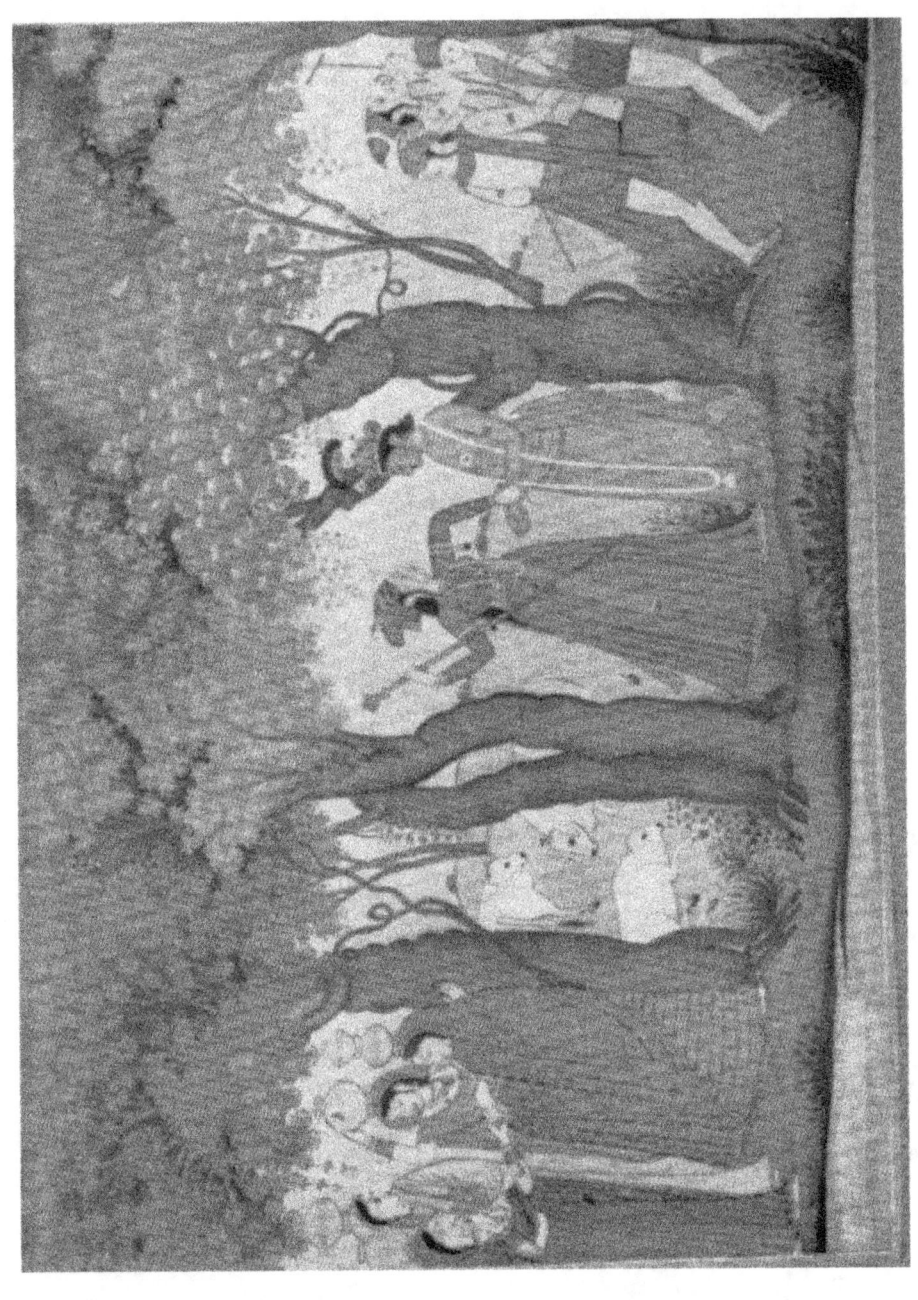

PLATE 35

Radha disguised as a Constable arresting Krishna as a Thief

Garhwal, Punjab Hills, *c.* 1785
Indian Museum, Calcutta

Tired of Krishna's attempts to waylay the cowgirls, Radha dons a turban, brandishes a constable's heavy staff and seizes Krishna by the wrist. 'I am a policeman of Raja Kansa, come to take you to gaol,' she says. The picture shows the cowgirls standing with their pitchers of curd, while cowherd boys—Krishna's accomplices—take to their heels. Krishna himself stands limply by, as if uncertain who the constable is.

The incident is unrecorded in the *Bhagavata Purana* but appears in later poetry as an instance of Radha and Krishna's mutual fun—teasing being an essential part of their love-making.

The picture is by the same master artist as Plate 19.

PLATE 36

Krishna meeting Radha

Illustration to a poem from the *Sat Sai* of Bihari
Kangra, Punjab Hills, c. 1790
N. C. Mehta collection, Bombay

An example of Krishna's meetings with Radha. Appearing as if by accident Krishna is lolling on his cowherd's stick while Radha, encouraged by a friend, has come to meet him. As she stands, there ensues that idyllic 'meeting of eyes' which Indian sentiment regarded as one of the most electrifying experiences in romance. In the picture, a tree pushes its flowering branches across open rolling slopes, suggesting by its fresh upsurgence the exquisite emotions stirring in Radha's and Krishna's hearts.

The picture is most probably by the Kangra artist, Kushala, to whom Plate 21 may also be assigned.

PLATE 37

Radha's Longing

Guler, Punjab Hills, *c.* 1810
Bharat Kala Bhawan, Banaras

In Indian painting and poetry, it was women driven to distraction by unappeased longing rather than men hungry with desire who formed the chief subject of romantic art. Pictures focussed on woman in all her varied moods and flattered the male mind by portraying her wilting with sadness when deprived of husband or lover.

The present picture shows Radha frenziedly contemplating her lonely state. Ornaments grown too hot for wearing—from the passion burning in her heart—are strewn about the bed, while hands tightly clasped suggest her wild unhappy torment. The vast and barren hills, empty angular buildings, tiny guttering candles and lonely flowering tree provide a sympathetic setting.

With its sinuous line and innocent delight in feminine form, the picture is typical of Guler painting at the start of the nineteenth century.

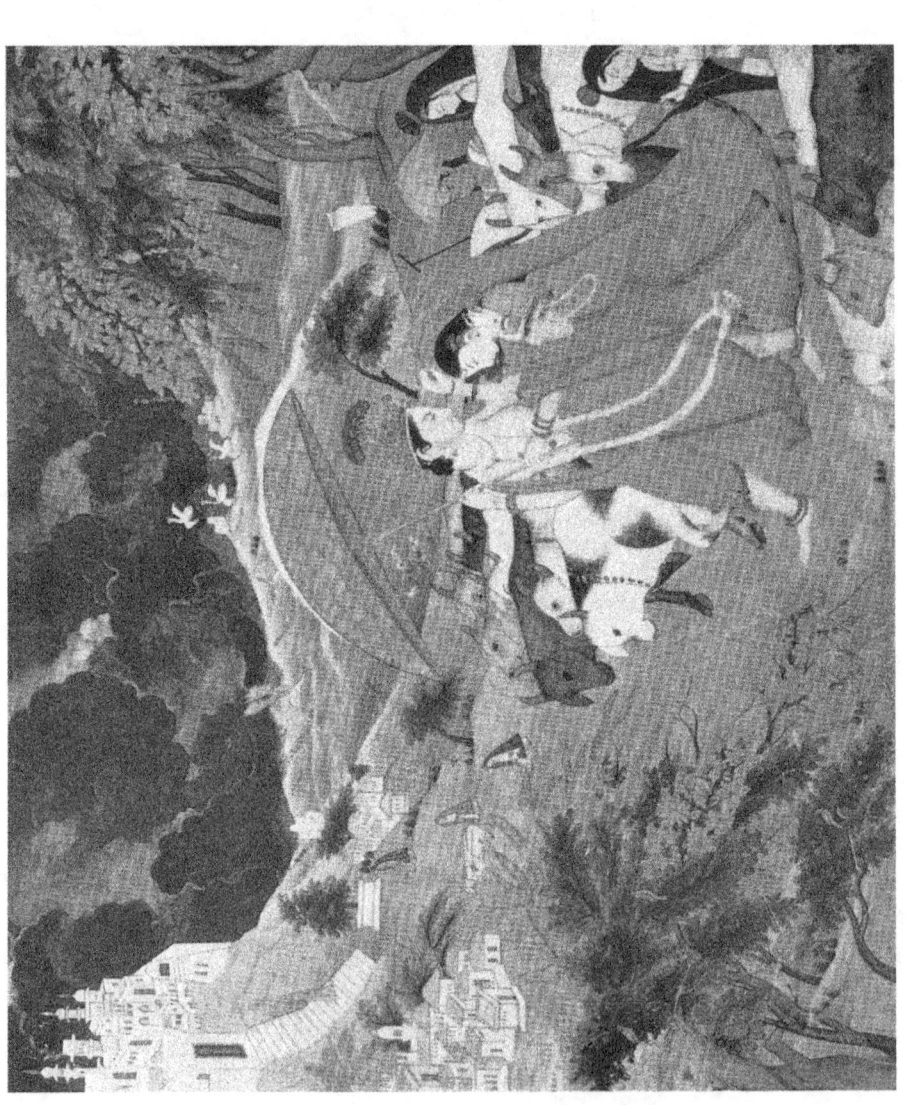

PLATE 38

Radha and Krishna returning in the Rain

Nahan, Punjab Hills, *c.* 1820
State Museum, Lahore,

A scene from Radha and Krishna's idyllic life together. Caught by a gale of wind and rain, the lovers are hurrying to shelter, Krishna carrying a leaf umbrella while cows and cowherds bend before the storm. In the distance, small figures wearing hooded cloaks hasten towards the village. Although keenly evocative of actual landscapes in the Punjab Hills— where palaces were usually set on rocky hill-tops with nearby villages clustering at their feet—the picture's main concern is to illustrate and interpret the lovers' feelings. The black clouds lit by eerie lightning and the trees tossing and swaying in the wind symbolize the passion raging in their hearts and suggest its ultimate outcome.

The picture represents a style of painting which is thought to have grown up at Nahan, the capital of Sirmur, after its neighbour, Garhwal, had been overrun by Gurkhas in 1804. Garhwal artists probably sought asylum at the Sirmur court and there developed a distinctive offshoot of the Garhwal manner.

PLATE 39

The Triumph of Radha

Kishangarh, Rajasthan, *c.* 1770
G. K. Kanoria collection, Calcutta

During the eighteenth century, Radha was often regarded as Krishna's permanent consort and was accorded divine honours—the present picture illustrating her final apotheosis. Seated together, their heads surrounded by haloes, the two lovers display their courtly charms. Krishna has now the mannered luxury of a high-born prince and Radha, no longer the simple cowgirl, is the very embodiment of aristocratic loveliness. As the lovers sit together, their forms offset by a carpet of lotus petals, Krishna attempts to put betel-nut in Radha's mouth—the gesture subtly indicating their loving intimacy.

SOURCES

Frontispiece. By courtesy of Victoria and Albert Museum, London, and of Messrs Faber and Faber.

1, 2. Hendley, *Memorials of the Jeypore Exhibition, IV, the RazmNamah.*

5. By courtesy of State Museum, Lucknow and of Mr. M. M. Nagar.

6, 12, 20, 28. Archeological Survey of India, New Delhi.

10, 19, 30, 33, 34. Victoria and Albert Museum, London.

18. Stchoukine, *La Peinture Indienne.*

22, 26, 31, 38. Messrs. A. C. Cooper Ltd, London.

23, 24. By courtesy of the Prince of Wales Museum, Bombay and of Dr. Moti Chandra.

25. *Journal of Indian Art*, Vol. XVI, 116.

27. By courtesy of Mr. M. S. Randhawa, I.C.S.

39. By courtesy of Mr. Gopi Krishna Kanoria.

3, 4, 7–9, 11, 13–17, 21, 29, 32, 35–37. Author's photographs.

For Product Safety Concerns and Information please contact our EU
representative GPSR@taylorandfrancis.com
Taylor & Francis Verlag GmbH, Kaufingerstraße 24, 80331 München, Germany

www.ingramcontent.com/pod-product-compliance
Lightning Source LLC
Chambersburg PA
CBHW052116300426
44116CB00010B/1688